THE EMPLOYEE EXPERIENCE SOLUTION

TRANSFORM EMPLOYEE ENGAGEMENT, IMPROVE WORKPLACE CULTURE, AND DRIVE RESULTS

MELISSA ANZMAN

LOOSEN YOUR WHITE COLLAR PUBLICATIONS

Published in the United States by Loosen Your White Collar Publications, Denver, Colorado.

ISBN 9781734681406

Dedicated to Simmy.
My favorite sidekick and writing buddy. You are my experience
differentiator every day.

CONTENTS

INTRODUCTION

Human Resources (HR) as a function is in the middle of a critical transition unlike any other it's experienced in the last 50 years. HR has transitioned from Personnel—a tactical, record-keeping focus to HR (a slightly more comprehensive department)—to where we are today. We are moving past HR into what's next: the employee experience. With much of the tactical HR work eventually being taken over by artificial intelligence (AI), the need for the current responsibilities of HR will no longer exist—but the gap of what's needed is even wider.

Over the past 15 years, as I looked at the various HR departments that I worked with, from Fortune 500 companies to 100-employee companies across the U.S., I realized that as a function, we've been following best practices and edicts from a narrow perspective and lens. The current generation of HR professionals were choosing this career path and realizing quickly that it wasn't right for them. They felt defeated, unmotivated, tired of the status quo, frustrated with the "seat at the table," "cover your ass," and "don't rock the boat" general consensus.

HR is losing key talent—future leaders—because we are so focused on these narrow perspectives and listening to gurus who haven't worked within an HR department in several decades. People who choose a career in HR have enormous depths of talent and drive. They hope to apply their talent effectively to help leaders make a positive impact, too. But engagement isn't the way in today's work environment: It's an outcome of the employee experience.

Employee engagement doesn't work. That has been proven. Even the people who have built their thought leadership careers on engagement are finally admitting to this—by "updating" their HR models and transformation guides. That's a great first step, but it still won't fix what's ultimately broken in the current state of HR.

I set out to learn as much as I could about why my own employee engagement efforts as an HR business partner failed dramatically. In one of my first global HR roles in 2009, I was partnered to provide HR support to the Global Marketing department—a dream assignment. When I started supporting them, their employee engagement score was 64%—not great, but better than the company's overall engagement score. And ready to make a huge impact, I went to work applying many of the so-called engagement best practices and 1,001 ways to improve it over the course of a year. I was committed and focused on all things engagement.

When the engagement survey came back the next year, I was beyond excited to see our results and how much we improved, only to find out that our score went *down* to 36%. Abysmal. I wanted to cry at my desk when I saw that number. Not only had all of the efforts we made not moved the needle, but they had crushed all of the engagement we had: lowering engagement well below what it was when we were doing nothing.

That's when my path to exploring what *really* works, started. And I started by using metrics to determine the right activities for us to focus on and which ones generated positive momentum. I noticed a pattern in what the metrics were telling us: Activities that improved the overall employee experience worked more effectively and more quickly than the tactical, "do this" ideas that are used more widely.

That realization led to a drastic change in how I operated as an HR business partner and leader.

The metrics told the story: Employee engagement is the wrong focus—an ineffective focus. We have 30 years of the same engagement rates to reinforce this. And very few people in the industry were listening, because engagement is what we've normalized with our C-suite, senior leaders, and, even now, employees. So HR professionals have continued to use "engagement" as a known focus, while our work centered around improving the employee experience. And the results spoke for themselves.

Now, the marketplace is starting to have rumblings about what's new and next, and the same thought leaders—who are still not HR practitioners—are leading us down the experience path, still seeing it through the engagement lens. That's not what this book is about.

This book isn't about HR. It's about leaders and how to build relationships among employees, leaders, and companies. The outcome? Better company results and truly engaged employees—because they are finding value and meaning in the work they do.

This is the employee experience—and it's not *another* HR "thing" or fad or the next coming of engagement. This is a holistic view on how effective companies work, and how HR and leaders come together to improve the lives of their employees and customers. It's not the future of work. It's fixing the way we're working today so that we can be successful now and in the future.

In this book you'll learn about what the employee experience is, how to use it to influence engagement and culture, and tactical ways to immediately increase your effectiveness as a leader. These strategies and tactics are for all leaders. Regardless of your department or level within the organization, you can apply these solutions right now, for immediate impact. Some exercises will require deep work on your behalf, and some will change management for you (and possibly your team) to reframe what you're currently doing to something more effective. You'll have the exact steps, tools, and framework to get you there.

During this process, you'll start to see things at work through a very different lens, and it may be uncomfortable as you identify various friction points or gaps. But it will be followed up with exactly how you can solve for those things with a proven strategy and the tactical components for some of the biggest projects, touchpoints, and milestones you'll come across during your career.

I'm excited to have you join me on this journey of pushing not only HR but leadership to the next level, giving us more control and influence over how we *can* change the lives of our employees—from candidate to alumni.

Work Has Changed—and it Won't Stop Changing

The world of work is constantly changing—and it has been, since the beginning of time. We're familiar with the big, sweeping changes that occurred during the Industrial Revolution or when Ford implemented the factory line, but there are continuous changes happening all the time.

While in HR we're usually part of influencing policy and expectations at work, we're also limited and constrained by the company we work for and the industry research we do. We can't possibly have a comprehensive worldview of how *much* work has changed and what's next on the horizon for the world of work. We see the changes we influence, but so many more are out there that we have experienced subconsciously or are *our* norm.

The other day at breakfast with my parents, my dad was telling me that "people don't stay with a company for 20+ years anymore. Instead of staying, if they don't get a promotion, they just jump to a new job."

Um, duh? That was my response, along with "Yep. That's what I've done my entire corporate career and why I jumped so much. Why would anyone stay with one company for 20 years anymore?" I went on to explain why that is the general mentality in today's corporate world—especially for Millennials and Gen Z.

It was clear to me that my dad, a Baby Boomer, was *really* late to this knowledge—and I talk to him about work all the time. It took him 10 years to actually *see* this as a work trend from his own perspective. This is how I approached my career even before it was the norm. (As a side note, I caught *a lot* of flak for my "job jumping" before it was cool.)

Another work trend that has dramatically changed the way we work is technology in general and telecommuting specifically. Most big companies are still trying to figure out if telecommuting or remote workers can work (and how to manage it), but there is no question that the opportunity has changed work and work opportunities.

The idea of being able to hire the absolute best talent, regardless of the physical location of your office, is enticing. For employees, the idea of being able to manage their own work schedule and environment a bit more is dreamy. As a side effect, we are also working longer hours, have the expectation to be responsive at all hours, and so on.

The point is, the way we work is constantly changing—and the way we're expected to deliver effective HR needs to change along with it.

I often tell the story about my first job in HR. It was a unique experience. I had just turned 25, and I had a manager title at a well-known Fortune 500 company in a small, highly coveted division. I wasn't working in HR until they couldn't find a home for my new department and—voilà—HR took me on. It is the catch-all department, right?

My boss, in her late 50s, had worked at this company her entire career and had been in HR for at least 20 years. She *knew* what HR meant to her employee population as defined by the company and her experience. I learned a lot from her, including the evolution of HR as a department.

She often shared how they did things before computers and copy machines (they had to write things out on triplicate paper; *what?!*), and of course my eyes were wide with shock. How could any work get done? I was very naïve and *young*. When she joined the "HR department," her role was more of a secretary. Then her department was named; they were finally fully formed as the Personnel department. As Personnel, they were responsible for the paperwork for each employee and ensuring employees were paid.

Things started to change dramatically in the Personnel department. In addition to paperwork and payroll, the department started to take on responsibility for tasks like recruiting and benefits management. It seems almost strange now that these things were often decentralized and inconsistent. And then, with computers, came (eventually) online and digital record management.

Boom! The employee engagement thing happened, and the role of HR was forever changed. According to my former boss, HR was suddenly responsible for delivering guidance, coaching, and more value to leaders and answering questions for employees. They were expected to be people and process experts to help their employees be productive.

HR changed not just because of technology changing, but the way companies viewed their employees changed. It sounds like a bit of an oxymoron in some ways, but instead of employees being thought of as "part of the family" or a "long-term investment" that rewarded a culture of joining a company and staying there for the employee's entire career, employees became a cost to company.

Yes, they were always a cost—and prior to this time employees were viewed as cogs in a machine in some ways. Employees became completely replaceable as a cost-savings effort. Today we think this way, particularly in larger companies, without questioning it. At the time, though, it was a huge change to the world of work.

And more importantly, it was a huge change in how Personnel and individual leaders were expected to manage their employees. We had to become knowledge experts while continuing to put the company's assets and costs first. It's a difficult balancing act (one we still teeter about today), but it was also a significant change in how our work environment changed. This creates a domino effect for so many other departments, policies, and expectations, and introducing engagement as the representation of productive employees.

Today's Employee Population

Just as the world of work, including norms and standards, is constantly changing, our employee population is forever changing. While there have always been several generations working at the same time, what's unique about our current, multigenerational workforce is not only the large number of generations due to people not retiring and people working earlier, but also the characteristics of each generation.

In today's multigenerational workforce, the need for customized or configurable experiences is the only way we can effectively capture each generation's attention. In the past, we have provided a standard one-size-fits-all experience—and our employees realigned their personal preferences to "get on board." Employees no longer feel the need to conform in this way. They want an experience that matches their preferences and will go to great lengths to achieve it.

Generations in the Workforce [1,2]

Generation	Traditionalists (pre–1945)	Baby Boomers (1946–1964)	Generation X (1965–1980)	Millennials (1981–1996)	Generation Z (1997–)
Workforce Population	2%	25%	33%	35%	5%

What does this mean to HR and leaders? The way we've been trying to engage employees—the motivation drivers, the rewards, the benefits, and the leadership—isn't effective to large swatches of our organization.

Recognizing this and helping our older two generations in the workforce (Boomers and Traditionalists) shift their perspective are not easy tasks. We are asking the same people who grew their corporate careers through a "get on board or lose your job" mentality to start talking about different options and approaches so people can slowly board the bus at their own pace. It can be frustrating and cause conflict —for employees in all generations.

While we're grappling with how to help different generations navigate the new engagement and experience needs, we still have to deliver an effective experience to *all* of our employees. That starts with understanding, more broadly, what each generation needs and wants within the framework, and how and *what* your company wants to deliver.

It's a decision point: Who does your company see as your primary employee audience (to speak to)?

Knowing that we can no longer capture our entire audience with one message and experience, our leaders (likely in one or two generations) will need to actively choose to focus the company's experience on a *different* generation. They'll decide that their own, "like me" audience will not be the company's primary target.

Looking at this more granularly, we're asking our senior leaders—part of the Traditionalist and Baby Boomer generations (with a few Gen X-ers thrown in)—to actively decide to change their messaging and experience to focus on Millennials (primarily) and Gen Z. It's not an easy task, but it's important to remember that generational differences in the workforce are not new. It feels exacerbated because the world of work has changed so much along with our current generational population, but this has forever been a problem to work through.

Going forward focused on the employee experience and creating our desired outcomes, it's important to remember your key audience focus for the experience—and who then becomes your secondary audiences—and to be aware of the friction points and obstacles you'll have to overcome from a generational perspective in message and implementation delivery.

The second part of the generation equation is understanding the mentality, needs, and desires of each generation, so you can focus your experience and engagement factors accordingly. One approach to this is to simply google the different generations and apply the stereotypes. While not the most recommended approach, it will at least provide you with some ideas on how each generation thinks from a stereotypical perspective.

You'll be missing out on the unique needs of your *company's specific generational audiences,* though. Those can be significant if you're trying to improve the experience for the human beings at your company.

The best way to craft different experiences for your different employee audiences is to talk to them directly. Use surveys and focus groups, and then testing out what is and isn't working.

We must be open to introducing new, different, and perhaps uncomfortable solutions that don't necessarily match our personal communication or delivery style. If we're going to create an experience that is truly effective, we have to get around our own personal biases— generational or experiential.

Once we have chosen our ideal experience audience/generation and understand what, specifically, they need and want—and how they want it delivered—we can move forward with the employee experience journey.

The "War" for Talent

In addition to our employee population being spread across several generations, and with the majority of our workforce being in a more "me-focused" generation when it comes to work options and choices, we also have an extremely tight talent pool to contend with. Employees, especially our key talent employees, know that they are in high demand. They have options.

What does this mean for you and your company?

It means that your employee experience is more critical than ever because your employees are not going to suck it up when they have a bad experience; they don't have to. Part of why employees job hop so much now is not only because the "golden handcuffs" have been removed across the board, but they also want work that works for them—not the other way around. We can partially attribute this to Millennials, which is a *good* thing, but *all* employees have realized that they don't need to put up with companies that deliver bad experiences on an ongoing basis.

When I wrote my first book, *Stop Hating Your Job: How to Be Happy at Work without Quitting*, in 2012, it was a purely selfish endeavor. I was tied to my current company at the time because of a large relocation bonus tie-back clause. I absolutely *loathed* my job. I can't say that strongly enough. I hated waking up each morning, I groaned during the entire commute, I stopped minding firing people (which I was flying around the country to do frequently), and the sound of my manager's voice grated on my last nerve. I was miserable—and in any other circumstance I would have already quit my job. Heck, I had an entire career of job hopping before then, so I'd never let myself hit this wall of complete and utter loathing. But I *couldn't* leave without a huge financial loss, which I was unwilling to take. So I figured out how to "suck it up, buttercup" for a set amount of time and turn my hate into a successful coping mechanism.

Today's workforce, as a whole, has the mentality I had in that situation. They have options out there, so it's a constant balancing act/question scenario: Do I care enough to suck it up and make it work here, or do I find a better fit?

Your employee experience is the main factor in this. Let me explain. You may absolutely love your job the majority of time (and if that's the case, I am so thrilled for you!). But think about a day you went to work in the best mood ever: The day was going to be great, you weren't packed with back-to-back meetings so you could actually *do* work, you were excited to focus on the projects you were going to dive into for the day . . . and then you received a totally annoying email from your boss or your client that ruined your plans for the day and made your blood boil for a minute. Of course, after that, you were *done*. Absolutely not feeling it for the day, not feeling your boss or client, not feeling your job or the company.

That, my friends, is how dramatic of an impact the employee experience can have on you personally—and on your employees. If you generally like your role, you take this as a bad day and roll with it. If you are unsure or are starting to dislike it, it's another notch of discontentment—the kind that leads our key talent to search for a new role.

We can't influence every email or bad client, but we can influence the overall experience people have with our company, our department, and our programs. If the general experience is positive, it takes more negative experiences to start shifting an employee from engaged to disengaged.

If we start out by creating an intentional employee experience that establishes a consistent way in which we want our employees to experience and interact with our company—including HR—we set the baseline of expectations and create meaningful and personal experiences throughout their journey. We amplify the positive, while helping diminish the negative experiences out of our control that erode our employees' desire to stay.

As leaders or as HR professionals or as employees, *we* have the opportunity and responsibility to create an employee experience that not only engages our employees to drive company results, but more importantly, to foster a safe and inclusive workplace environment. Throughout this book, I will share how empowered we are to change our workplace by slightly shifting our focus from employee engagement solutions to creating small, positive moments (and removing friction points) for employees throughout their employment and interaction with our culture.

WHAT IS THIS THING—THE EMPLOYEE EXPERIENCE?

Over the past few years, as HR has embarked on the next H(R)evolution, HR has continued to look for ways to expand beyond employee engagement to deliver a more cohesive and comprehensive employee experience. Employee engagement is no longer working. **It's not delivering what is needed in today's work environment.**

Companies are constantly searching and struggling to find and keep talent who have the right skills—and who want to grow their careers with them. Historically, HR has been tapped to lead the charge of delivering talent into the pipeline through recruiting efforts and then retaining that talent through employee engagement surveys and actions, followed closely by learning and development for growth opportunities.

And while HR has been following this roadmap, employee engagement rates have stayed the same for the last 30 years. According to Gallup's 2017 State of the Global Workplace study, only 15% of employees are engaged in the workplace around the world. In the U.S., that number is 33%. Though double the global average, the U.S. percentage has also remained steady for the past 30 years.

In Gallup's August 2018 employee engagement survey[3], the top-line finding was engagement was on the rise in the U.S.—increasing from 33% to 34%, which tied the highest level of engagement in the poll's history, which began in 2000. A 1% increase was celebrated, when in reality, there has been no significant change. The poll also indicated that the percentage of employees who are "actively disengaged" is 13%, while the remaining employees in the "not engaged" category is at 53%. What does this mean for the state of employee engagement across the U.S.—and at your company? That while perhaps a third of your employees are engaged, the rest are actively disengaged or don't care and are at risk. It's this population— the 66% or so—who will react more strongly to negative employee experiences, leading to turnover.

At same time, companies are struggling to find talent to replace disengaged workers, especially when there is a higher need of skilled labor than available talent. According to Monster's 2019 State of Recruiting survey[4], 62% of the recruiters surveyed says it's harder to find quality candidates than it was just five years ago. The skills gap between the talent companies need to run efficient businesses compared to available talent, is a real concern for those who recruit. According to a SHRM survey[5], 83% of HR professionals struggled finding suitable candidates between mid-2018 and 2019. It's becoming more difficult to find the right talent, especially for highly skilled professionals. As leaders, we feel disengagement from our employees in an ongoing basis: performance concerns, tardiness, attendance, handholding for tasks, low participation rates, and more.

Why does this even matter? In addition to the human impact (burnout, frustration, job-hopping, decreased productivity and more), disengaged employees cost organizations about $450–550 billion each year in the U.S. alone.[6] That is with our current employee engagement rate around 34%—the highest number we've achieved in 30 years! As the State of the Global Workplace numbers indicate, clearly our current path isn't working. And our approach has the opportunity to do more harm than good in today's global work environment, as companies and HR have spent $720 million[7] on employee engagement software and solutions, only to be at the same engagement levels as when we started measuring engagement.

This is why it's time to shift our focus from our current path of engagement into what today's workforce is desperately seeking: a career that's more than just a job—an experience.

I define employee experience this way: **all of the ways in which your employees interact with your company, leaders, and Human Resources, leading to one consistent, pre-defined experience.** This experience shapes each employee's perspective about the company as a whole, including their personal attachment/loyalty, engagement, motivation, drive, and desire.

Your employee experience is more than just two or three components. It includes all of the mini-moments, touchpoints, and impressions throughout your employees' lifecycle. In its ideal state, your employee experience is intentional, and it aligns and reinforces your company's culture, brand, mission, and core values.

When considering this definition, it's a huge bucket—one that, when examined at a macro level, is overwhelming to say the least. But like all big rocks, this isn't something that you can create or fix at the macro level. Instead, employees experience your company through micro touchpoints of culture, interactions, successes, friction points, and everyday work.

Consider this: To help you better understand the employee experience, think back to the last job you landed and consider the entire process. Did it leave you with a good impression of the company? Did the online application make you want to pull out your hair? Did you feel like you were working with professional recruiters who were knowledgeable, helpful, and your ally? Was the process timely, or did it drag on for ages? Was it easy to evaluate the offer and learn more about the company's benefits, perks, and culture?

And once you joined the company, what was your onboarding experience like? Again, did it make you more excited about accepting the position, or did it make you start to worry that you made a terrible choice? Were you warmly welcomed or left to fend for yourself? And what about the technology component: Did you have a computer, login information, a phone, and so on? How quickly were you able to start working, receive training, and get started?

We can parse out each and every step within the employee lifecycle and ask these hard questions to determine how seamless your employee experience actually is.

This is how every HR team member helps create the lifecycle experience. One small roadblock along the way, can have a significant and long-lasting impact for the employee and your company. One nugget of doubt, of questioning, of frustration, or of annoyance can easily flip the switch for an employee from engaged to disengaged. With its broad scope and impact in delivery, the employee experience cannot be owned by one department alone. It's a partnership between HR and leaders—with a shared plan and consistent delivery.

The good news is, creating a cohesive employee experience is not *another* new thing that HR has to take on. Rather, it's a joint effort shared among HR, leaders, and the company itself (which as employees, we don't have the ability to influence on our own)—with HR leading the experience by first being intentional with how HR delivers continuous value and an ROI for the company.

WHAT DOES HR OWN IN THE EMPLOYEE EXPERIENCE?

HERE'S AN IMPORTANT THING TO REMEMBER, SO WE DON'T MAKE THE same mistakes we made with employee engagement: This is not something that HR owns peripherally and then passes off to unskilled leaders to influence action and change. That has failure written all over it.

Instead, the employee experience is something that HR owns. Full stop.

You (as in HR) owns the experience by default because you influence each and every step along the journey. You are responsible for all things people and culture—and the employee experience sums up both.

With that ownership comes not only a lot of responsibility, but also some apprehension—because HR as a whole and individual HR practitioners don't necessarily have the skill set currently to deliver this effectively. And just like previous skill sets that have been thrust on HR (or any other department, as the world of work is in a continuous state of change), it will feel uncomfortable as we learn our way through it.

This book will help you do just that—and clearly define the skills and ownership throughout the employee experience, so you can get ahead of the learning curve and deliver immediate value.

As part of HR's ownership classification, in traditional project management terms, you are the project sponsor. You get to create the employee journey and the roadmap to deliver an effective employee experience, bringing in the various touchpoints and components along the way to ensure your employees are at the center of experience decisions.

But HR can't deliver the employee experience on their own.

Big sigh of relief, right?

HR owns the experience, but the components are owned by HR and several other partners across the organization. You are not now responsible for *everything* that employees come across. **Your area of influence hasn't shifted with ownership, but the responsibility has.** For instance, HR still owns the recruiting process, so that will be one component that HR will continue to own and be responsible. And it is also a component of the employee experience.

Consider the employee experience the framework for how all things HR fit together as a whole. Right now, the only idea cobbling HR activities, technology, deliverables, and so forth together is that (a) the "thing" is people-related or (b) there wasn't a "clean owner" for that thing back when it was originally assigned.

That's why, still today, it's unclear if HR should sit under Operations, Legal, or Shared Services; be its own entity reporting to the CEO; or be any other nebulous home in which your current HR department resides. For the record, it should be its own entity reporting directly to the CEO—and the Employee Experience Framework will help convince your leadership team that's the case if it's not already there.

We've grown and shifted from being paper pushers and the department where "careers went to die" to taking on whatever someone thought we should do to fill a need. This is not going to be successful for creating an effective employee experience.

This brings us back to the case for your experience as your people framework—what ties all HR-related activities together with one common outcome and purpose.

You own the framework and will continue to own the various elements along the way. But you don't own everything.

2

WHAT DO LEADERS OWN IN THE EMPLOYEE EXPERIENCE?

THERE IS NO FEASIBLE WAY FOR HR TO OWN THE ENTIRE EMPLOYEE experience and related touchpoints, systems, and outcomes. This is similar to what HR realized about five years into the employee engagement project: HR is a separate group, having some influence, but not the most important part of an employee's everyday work experience.

When HR acknowledged that engagement wasn't something that they could create on their own, the way most HR departments moved forward was to split the responsibility. HR would own the survey—and pass *everything else* back to the leaders to magically solve for the company. We know this wasn't effective, either.

Using those lessons, the employee experience is more of a joint venture or partnership between HR and leaders at all levels. For this partnership to be successful, we have to create an inclusive and collaborative relationship to not only deliver the right experience but also to ensure those responsible for delivering action and change have the skill set and knowledge to do so.

So while HR owns the framework and the overall project, each leader (for our purposes, this is defined as a people leader at any level) must contribute to the employee experience project as well.

Leaders will partner with HR to deliver the activities that are outlined in areas outside of HR's purview. And being that leaders are the people closest to each employee, they also are responsible for ensuring that the experience works as defined.

What does this mean exactly?

It means that leaders have their own deliverables and activities along the employee experience—ways in which they are able to influence, reinforce, and deliver across the employee journey. They are responsible for delivering these activities in a way that aligns with the overall experience goals and provide support and ongoing feedback about the experience.

HR and leaders need to work together to define the roles and responsibilities clearly—and know that they will continue to evolve and change over time, so that the experience isn't an activity the employee endures in different silos.

Leaders own the success of the experience. If the roadmap doesn't deliver as it's supposed to, various friction points are encountered, there are gaps in the process, unforeseen delays, or impressions that are inconsistent, leaders are the ones who will ensure things get back on track.

You may be thinking that all leaders are not created equal—and that, if we're talking about leaders being people leaders at any level, we may have too many cooks in the kitchen. You're right.

Leaders—at all levels—have the same level of ownership to the above outlined delivery of the experience. But senior leaders (leaders who are first-, second-, or third-level direct reports of the CEO) have additional responsibility. Senior leaders are responsible for shaping, with HR, the desired employee experience: the high-level plan of *what* the desired employee experience needs to be, in order to be successful and align with the company's goals, mission, values, and success factors.

The delivery of the experience, though, is consistent across the board for leaders—regardless of senior leadership designation (or not).

THE EMPLOYEE EXPERIENCE JOURNEY

A THOUSAND MOMENTS OVER THEIR LIFECYCLE

WHEN WE EXAMINE THE EMPLOYEE EXPERIENCE AS A WHOLE, IT'S larger than just one experience, interaction, or touchpoint, suspended in a point in time. Instead, it's how thousands of moments come together for each individual employee across their employment lifecycle with an employer.

The employee experience starts even before your employees becomes an employee. It starts when they decide to apply for a role and become a candidate and continue through their alumni employment experience.

Evaluating the experience more broadly is more accurately aligned with how people think and feel about a company and/or brand.

Consider this: What is your favorite restaurant? Why is it your favorite? How did you first discover it? Does it have a menu that excites you? Is the ambiance perfect? Is the food dang good every time you eat there? Or is the service amazing? Do you tell others about this place?

For me, it's a neighborhood Mexican restaurant. I heard about it from an online "Best Of" list and decided to try it. The food is delicious and spicy, and consistent. The service isn't fantastic, but it's good enough, and we're never left to fend for ourselves. The ambiance is casual and easy. These are all things I love when I want my favorite cuisine.

I will try just about any restaurant once—but if there's poor service, or if the food is bad, or if the prices are crazy high, I won't return. Those aren't the customer experiences I'm willing to put up with to enjoy a meal.

We all have different things that excite us about our favorite restaurants—and experiences that tell us never to go back to a place where we have a bad experience. All of these touchpoints create the experience we have as customers at our favorite (or least favorite) restaurant.

The same is true about where you work. You view your overall experience at a company as the sum total of many interactions that create the overall feeling and experience for you—and that will always be uniquely different than the overall feeling and experience of the person sitting next to you. It's also why there can be a spectrum of opinions on how great or terrible a company is: because we each evaluate our experience through our own preferences.

This is why, if you want to create a cohesive employee experience, it's critical that you understand that the experience itself begins when a candidate decides to take a chance on your company (when they are interested enough to apply) and follows them well after they have left your company.

This the employee experience journey: the thousands of small and big moments that make up your employee's experience across their lifecycle.

Reflection: Your Employee Experience Journey
Consider a previous employer and your own experience as an employee at various stages.

Potential Candidate: Why did you join that company—or even apply for a role there—in the first place? Were you a referral?

Did you find the role on a job board and it sounded interesting? Was the potential for growth at the company intriguing? Were you excited about their total rewards offering? What attracted you to the company?

Candidate: When you were going through the recruiting (interviewing) process, what was your impression overall? Did you feel attracted to, repelled by, or neutral about the company? Did the recruiting process feel long, short, incomplete, just right?

Pre-Employee: When you accepted the offer, how was your onboarding experience? What were you telling your friends about your new company and role? Were you excited? Did you feel ready?

Employee: When you started, did you have all of the tools and information you needed to be successful? Was it easy to sign up for benefits and direct deposit information?

Tenured Employee: As time went on, how did your feelings about the company grow and change? What things started to annoy you or make you really happy?

Alumni: How was your exit process? Did you leave on good terms? How do you feel about your company now? Is it the same or different than how you felt about it at the previous stages in the lifecycle? Would you recommend your former employer to your friends?

THE EVOLUTION OF THE EXPERIENCE

IN EARLY 2016, JACOB MORGAN, AN AUTHOR ON THE FUTURE OF work, widely shared his vision for the employee experience on his website and in his book *The Employee Experience Advantage*. This was one of the first introductions of the experience concept and was helpful in pushing the employee engagement factor to the next level, by focusing on a broader concept.

Morgan's employee experience is defined by three components: culture, technology, and physical space. These add up to determine an employer's employee experience equation. It's important to note that his equation was created to help "win the war for talent" by using these three components to create work environments in which candidates and employees alike want to work.

While this definition has been so helpful in pushing us to focus more broadly on the experience, providing more measurable and tangible ways for HR to focus and deliver better experiences, this narrow definition does not reflect how employees experience work today—nor how they will in the future. It's a great foundation, but it's not inclusive.

For example, even in the few years since Morgan's book was

published, the technology and physical space standards have changed drastically (not to mention the types of cultures employees want). Tech has continued to get easier to interact with, do more things, provide different interfaces and modes of use, and so on. And these solutions, particularly on the HR tech side, continue to be broken, even after three years of deeply investing in them, spending more to create a great tech experience, and trying to become more tech-savvy organizations.

As for how physical workspaces have changed, how many companies are pushing for a more remote workforce? Closing their onsite locations? Moving things offshore? Changing their office space models—including hot-desking (claiming a desk when you show up), open plans to closed plans—and back again, pods, and more?

Physical workspaces have become more about flexible work options than actual work environments. And with that, there's a new item of focus: work process, flow, and self-management (along with the various virtual team technology now needed, and management skills to ensure work is still getting done).

In other words, these three areas of focus Morgan outlines are still important, but the world we work in today is rapidly changing and these areas aren't able to capture the experience on their own, nor are they necessarily applicable to companies of all sizes.

This is why I believe it's necessary to expand the employee experience definition to include components that are less restrictive and more applicable to today's work environments, employee populations, and the future of HR. We will build on this foundation. The experience itself is applicable to deliver more than winning the war on talent. It will do that, but also ensure you're retaining your talent once you've onboarded them, helped them grow their careers, and provided them with a positive impression, so they become brand ambassadors even after they leave.

THE EMPLOYEE EXPERIENCE FRAMEWORK

BECAUSE THE EMPLOYEE EXPERIENCE IS VAST AND WE'RE MOVING beyond three standard areas to review (culture, technology, and physical space), we need a standard way to capture the employee experience journey—to make it easier for you to influence engagement through quantitative and qualitative measures.

The Employee Experience Framework is made up four components: Know, Feel, Act, Touch.

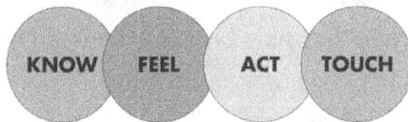

This framework may feel a bit different than most HR models you're used to. It's about your employee first, and how we can create the ideal journey for them—not about us in HR. By putting our employees at the center of this model, we instantly change the focus of our work to be centered on their journey.

Storytelling for HR™

Before we go deeper into the framework and its components, it's important to share why this model is so different and so successful. To do that, I'm going to bring you back to your high school English class. For some, this may be a fond memory. Or perhaps this is the first time you're remembering it. Either way, let's talk about storytelling.

Why do we need to consider storytelling when we're talking about HR? Because in order to *influence* our employees and have our work deliver *real value*, we need to shift the way we approach our employee-focused work. And storytelling is the easiest way to explain this.

In a story's framework, there are a set of standard characters that help move the story along. You will see these same character archetypes in books, movies, successful marketing campaigns, podcasts, and more.

From a character perspective, every story has a:

- *Hero:* the person you're rooting for to succeed. You may not like the person, but you keep reading or watching to find out what happens.
- *Guide:* the person or narrator who helps guide the hero to success. They know a lot more than the hero, they see everything, and they help bring the hero along their journey.
- *Villain:* the person, place, or thing that gets in the way of the hero achieving success. The villain creates friction and the ultimate feeling of reward and success when the hero overcomes it.

Traditionally in HR or employee-focused communications, we throw these rules out the window. We insert "corporate speak" about what we think the employee needs to know and do, add a bit of legalese and some HR acronyms to spice things up, and call it a good communication. I've seen this across companies of all sizes over the past 15 years.

We all know that it doesn't work. Our employees have stopped caring or even taking the employee engagement surveys we send out. They have more questions than feasible about their benefits—even though all of the details are available. And when we try to incite action, it feels like it takes a force of nature.

It's because we're ignoring the story framework.

When we look at each character, here is what we see by default and how it looks like when it's successful. Think current state versus future state of our HR view.

Character	Current State	Success State
Hero	HR. We are trying to achieve our desired outcomes, goals, actions, etc.	Employee. They are taking the desired actions to be successful on their journey.
Guide	HR. We are trying to tell them what they need to do, how they need to do it. and by when they need to accomplish it.	HR. As the experts, we show the hero why getting to the end is important for their overall success: we're guiding and supporting them along their journey with a hero-focused perspective.
Villain(s)	Employee. Why won't they do what we want them to do? Budget. If we had more money, we could fix this problem Boss/senior leadership. Don't they get that this isn't working?	The problem, friction point, or danger we're helping our hero avoid.

Figure: Character Roles

Let's dive deeper into these roles. Changing your story focus will have an immediate impact on the success of your employee experience journey, your communications, and your HR programs. And you implement it starting right now.

Hero

In our current state, HR sits as the hero of the story. We're constantly trying to have our employees achieve *our* goals and action steps. It's about what *we* need *them* to do or take action on, so that X [insert outcome or goal here]. Yes, we know that, for example, enrolling in benefits is for the employees' own interests, but we don't approach it that way. Instead, we say things like: "Annual Enrollment is Nov. X–Nov. Y. You need to enroll by this date. No exceptions will be made." While this is a generally true statement, it's about HR: We're stating facts and action items as they relate to *us,* not at all about our employees.

An easier way to think about this shift is to think about your kids (or if you don't have kids, your siblings, parents, best friend, whomever). How many times have you said, "Do this or else" or "You should . . ." or "Stop that right now!"? How many times out of a hundred were you successful in them *doing* that action or heeding your "advice"?

Likely almost never. And it's because *you* were being the hero of the story in your approach. And we all have a little rebel inside of us that will fight this because **we want to be the hero of our own story.**

Had you shifted the language to "I've noticed that you don't seem to be getting the results you're hoping for by doing X. Maybe consider Y as a different approach?" or "You don't seem to be behaving in a way to earn your allowance this week. Perhaps you can pause and find a better way to get your sister's attention?"

Yes, these statements are more thought-out than in-the-moment rants, but they are effective. They work because, instead of the command coming from you as the hero, the command is being heard by the other person as something that will benefit *them* and move them forward along their own hero journey.

Guide

One person, group, or entity cannot be both the hero on a journey and the all-knowing guide. It's impossible, as one is in the moment experiencing things, and the other knows everything and brings the hero along for the ride. If we simply shift our focus from trying to be both at the same time and let our employees be the hero, we can live in the guide role.

As the guide currently, we are fulfilling this role by, more or less, barking orders at our employees—nicely, of course, but our approach is to tell them what they need to do and how they need to do it. It's easy for us to approach things this way because it's the most direct way to communicate things.

But it doesn't *help* our heroes on their journey.

How many times have you been given a project and then told exactly how you had to go about it, every step along the way, how to complete things in a specific document, and so on? I've been guilty of assigning things this way—many times. Do this, but do it *my way,* and if you're not, even if the end result is the same, I'm never going to let you do anything new/fun again!

Sound familiar? Not only is that micromanaging from a delegation perspective, but it's micromanaging our employee outcomes and their journey, too!

As a guide, our role is to place breadcrumbs, so to speak, along the path so our employees know where they need to go—but to let them get there in a way that works for them. A very easy way to do this is to provide different communication channels to deliver information and knowledge. Let your employees find the path that matches their learning style and also helps them realize *they* get to choose.

If your company is struggling with employee accountability or decision-making, it usually has to do with the guide (at the company, in

HR, leadership, etc.) not *guiding*. Our employees have instead been trained to be followers. They aren't able to hop on the journey and make decisions or be accountable, because we have told them exactly what and how to do things for so long.

Being the guide is all about showing a pathway to success and letting our hero walk along the path.

Villain

We all need an adversary of sorts—not necessarily an evil adversary or villain, but something to be a counterpoint to our path. In our current state, our villains tend to be more negative and things we can't influence or change (without finding a new job).

It's easy to rally against our employees who won't just take the dang action we have told them to or provided them resources for; it's easy to look at our lack of funds or having the wrong technology to be the solver of all problems; and it's *really* easy for us to place our boss and/or senior leaders at the heart of everything that is wrong in our job. But we can't influence change with those villains. They are still going to be there; they are still going to be the "obvious" reasons why things aren't as successful as they can be.

In our future state, our villain is not evil. The villain consists of specific issues, problems, and friction points that we can solve. It is still an adversary, but by our story definition, a villain is something we can overcome and succeed against.

If you approach your villains with this lens, you will not only be happier at work in general (because, honestly, who wants to continue to hate on things we can't change?), but you will also help your hero succeed in their journey because you will all be able to succeed and influence outcomes.

In general, you can see a big difference between our current approach and a storytelling approach with regard to creating impactful experiences and communications. (It's applicable to both!) In our current state, we start from our own perspective within HR, and by doing so we take on a losing proposition before we even start. We're trying to get our employees to think and act like we do—when they have no idea what's going on. They're joining us in the middle of the story. All our employees know is that they need to do something because *someone* is telling them to, but they don't want to. So instead of taking the action we want them to, they end up throwing a temper tantrum—rebelling against our request. Internally, they are rallying against taking action or giving the experience grace, because they don't understand why it matters to them, specifically.

Let's look back at our restaurant example from earlier in the chapter. What if you go to your favorite restaurant, but this time the owner tells you what you will be eating (because it is their favorite dish; it doesn't matter if you have any allergies), they give you the exact timing of when you will be finished with your meal, and they kick you out when that time is up (even if you're not done eating). How would you feel about *that* experience compared to how you were feeling before? It's constraining—and you'd likely pick a different restaurant next time.

That's because your favorite restaurant sees you as a customer. Through that lens, they have built an entire dining experience around you. You are the hero. You get to enjoy a nice meal! Your server, chef, and owner are your guides, helping you choose great food, delivering good service, supporting you, and serving you on your dining journey. Your hunger is the villain. You must slay it with yummy food. The décor and ambiance even play a role in creating the setting and environment for your experience to unfold.

Restaurants, without you overtly knowing they are doing it, create a storytelling experience for you.

By shifting our storytelling focus to our employees and considering them your customers in the employee experience journey, you will already have created a more successful journey. Because you have placed your employees in the hero's seat, you are setting them up for a journey, seeking out success.

With this new storytelling construct in mind, let's dive deeper into the elements that comprise the Employee Experience Framework.

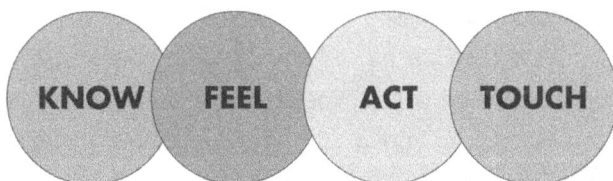

KNOW FEEL ACT TOUCH

Know

The employee experience journey begins with Know.

Know is applied in two different contexts along the journey:

1. **What do our employees need to know, and**
2. **What do our employees need?**

At first glance, these two questions appear to be the same. But they are very different.

The first question is about what you—as the company, leader, or HR—need to share with your employee at that moment of the journey. Perhaps it's an update, a legal requirement, an action they need to take, or an activity that helps them feel connected. Whatever the Know is, the first question is about the company—the guide.

This part of the question is the what: what *we* have to share for knowledge to be receive.

The second question is about what your employees need. It's focused on the hero of the story. It's about supporting their overall knowledge, learning, success, engagement, and overall experience.

This part of the question is the why: why it's important for your employee to know that item along the journey. This is the personal connection for each employee, bringing understanding to the interaction point.

Question 1: What Do Our Employees Need to Know?

Currently, we tend to approach the activities, campaigns, and employee-focused actions based on what we've done historically or some trendy advice that we picked up a recent conference. It's the "rinse and repeat" method or the "looking over the shoulder" method. Using either method, we move into implementation without little intention—and then wonder why our rollout, communication, or activity wasn't as successful as we hoped it would be.

So we need to pump the brakes instead of moving to implementation mode.

In order to clearly define the experience we want our employees to have, we have to start with what we want our employees to know and learn at each step along the way. Since we know the experience is expansive and can be overwhelming, we apply this intention at the micro level, asking at each interval along the way: What does our employee need to know?

Defining what they need to know is also the first step in determining whether the activity, campaign, action, or other employee activity, is even necessary.

Gasp! Why would we stop doing something we're already doing and have socialized our employees about?

Perhaps you're thinking about the last mediocre campaign you delivered or the last employee engagement survey or the previous talent management review cycle. You know it wasn't awesome, but you have to do it because you've been doing it year after year. Right?

Know is the first place for you to consider the value that the activity is delivering—and to determine if you should continue it.

If you cannot answer with absolute certainty that there is something that your employees *need to know* about that activity at that point in their journey, then it doesn't deliver any specific value to your employee population. It can be a big knowledge nugget that's needed, or a small one, but it must have a purpose to remain on the journey.

Question 2: What Do Our Employees Need?

It's usually easier for us to determine the **what** in the Know equation (question 1), but we tend to not consider the **why** for our employees—which is the most critical element for inducing action and influencing the desired experience.

To know what our employees need, we must understand their motivation at that point and why it's important for *them* to know what we're trying to tell them.

Historically, since we have placed ourselves as the hero of the story, we communicate the Know section with a focus on what we are trying to share. The communication becomes all about us, which leaves us struggling from the very beginning, because we are speaking *at* our employees, not with them.

By moving our employees to the hero position in our story, we, as the guide, are able to reframe the conversation. In doing so, we focus on what the employee cares about, rather than what we want to talk about.

This is a big shift, so let's review a couple of examples.

Know in Action

This is the message sent to new employees on day one of their employment at a company that employees 85,000 worldwide.

> Welcome to the company! You will get access to your company log-in information, including your email account, within the next three business days. Until then, please work with your manager to complete your onboarding plan and review your new hire sessions on our learning portal here.

This message includes some of the standard information new employees receive from most companies: a welcome, access info, and next steps. But when reviewing this example, do we see the **Know** elements?

What do our employees need to know? And what do our employees need?

In this message, the company needed to tell their new employee just a few things: a quick welcome to acknowledge their new employee status; a time line update on system access; where to go to ask questions from here; and a reminder to complete their new hire onboarding sessions.

In general, this message shared these details with the new hire, delivering (albeit a bit mediocrely) the **what.**

However, that's where the message stops. There is absolutely nothing about what that new employee needs—and definitely not **why.**

From the employee perspective, what impression did this email leave? Did it create the interaction that a new hire would be excited about? Would they feel connected to the company and excited to get started?

In short, *no* to all of the above. This was a push message all about sharing details the company wanted the new hire to know, not utilizing the opportunity to engage the employee.

To create a better message, we need to shift the message to include more why. Here's how, using the same base message:

Welcome to the company. We're so excited you've decided to **grow your career here** and we can't wait **to partner with you on all the great things we can do together!**

Our system set-up process takes a bit of extra time **to ensure we have everything ready for you and properly assigned as soon as you get access,** so please bear with us as we work through all of the details. You will have your log-in credentials within the next three business days—which will include access to your email account and all related systems.

These details will be delivered to you at your personal email address, to maintain confidentiality. **If you experience any issues with your system access,** or your details don't arrive within three business days, please contact IT at help@company.com.

In the meantime, **to help welcome you to our company and learn about our culture and more about what we do,** we have created some new hire virtual trainings on our learning portal.

Don't worry, **you don't need your system access to start viewing these.** Just your name, start date, and manager info will get you started.

And of course, **your manager has been eagerly anticipating your arrival and has created a plan to help you onboard, learn your role, meet your team members, set relevant goals, get your administrative stuff taken care of, and ensure your overall success.**

Welcome aboard. We're excited to have **you as our newest team member.** Our team members are our **biggest asset**—so if you ever run into any issues, have a question, or want to send along a suggestion, please do so at awesome@company.com.

And don't forget to log on to our learning portal to start your onboarding training. You can do so by clicking this link here.

Cheers!
HR, SVP

Other than the obvious of the second message being longer, there are several **whys** included this time (the bolded text in the message). Through the new employee's lens, when you read the updated message, you feel connected with the company and the experience. You know why certain things are set up as they are; you feel a part of the company already—and that they have been excited for you, specifically, to start; there is a plan in place and stop-gaps if you have any issues; and we've interspersed the items we need our employees need to know with why it's important to them to know these things.

We move from spewing information *at* our employees, to creating a conversation with them.

This is what happens when you are able to combine both parts of **Know** within an employee experience journey point.

Let's take a look at another example.

Company B is a publicly traded company with 4,000 U.S. employees and an additional 1,000 employees worldwide. They have an HR operating model that reports directly to the CEO, with the transaction work through a self-service portal and HR business partners supporting specific business groups remotely. They have a semi-shared services model for key HR areas including recruiting, benefits, and employee relations.

Company B is evaluating their employee experience journey, as their employee engagement numbers haven't been moving much in the past three years, and they have had an abnormally high turnover rate (particularly within their key talent ranks) over the same time period.

To create their Employee Experience Framework, we start with the company view of what we want the overall experience to be.

Their "Know"

What do our employees need to know?

Our employees need to know that we offer a great place to grow their careers and truly invest in our people. Our internal promotion rate is 32%; our average learning rate has increased from 15 hours per employee per year to more than 40 hours per employee per year; and we are innovative—not only with our external customer solutions, but also with our internal tools.

We have an outstanding total rewards program that has been developed with a multi-generational focus, we hire for knowledge and talent—and invest in our hires, we encourage open-door leadership, and we expect our leaders to be inclusive and operate with a self-management style.

We serve the top 10% companies on the Fortune 500, and our customer service has been rated the highest in our industry for the past five years and counting.

What do our employees need?

Our employees need: a truly inclusive and safe work environment; leaders who encourage learning and growth; clearly set expectations and success factors; and total rewards that support their lives outside of work, meet them at every stage of their career, and deliver an outstanding value.

What We Can Learn

This is a snapshot of Company B's Know—after a lot of work narrowing down what was most important for the company and their employees. It may read to you like a list of stats or a copying of core values, both of which are factors in the Know section. But that's not *all* that comprises this section.

And remember: This is to capture their overall employee experience. We can also apply this on a more micro level when we evaluate the various touchpoints on the roadmap, identifying what our employees need to know in their onboarding email, for example, or what they need during annual enrollment, and so on.

Before moving on to the next element, be sure your Know statement has been clearly defined. You've outlined exactly what your employees need to know and what they need. Once you've done this, you can move into the second element of the Employee Experience Framework: Feel.

Feel

Feel is the stage where we define how we want our employees to feel at that specific point in time—in relation to the company and their overall experience.

Stick with me. I know that, for many, even the *thought* of adding an emotional component to any working model will make you roll your eyes or run away as fast as you can. (I tend to fall into that camp too.) In this model, though, Feel is not adding in a layer of woo. Instead, it's intentionally deciding on the type of connection we want our employees to have.

In order to build the ideal experience, we have to establish a relationship with our employees, and then build and reinforce it throughout the journey. If we leave out the intention behind Feel, our relationship-building will lack cohesiveness.

If we look at the Feel factor through the storytelling lens, Feel will mirror the emotions the hero of the story (your employees) is experiencing along the way. These are the elements that suck us in as readers. They are what make us invested enough in the outcome to follow the hero throughout the rest of the novel.

Here's an important thing to note: The journey *should* be different at each step. It's our way, as the guide, to frame our work to deliver our desired experience consistently, across time. It's how we influence the various steps, touchpoints, and activities along the way.

We use feel to ensure we capture the emotion we want our employees to actively have: creating meaningful connection to the company, not just checking the box through various actions.

Feel in Action

Let's use the same example as we did in the Know in Action

section and dive into the Feel elements for their onboarding message. This company wanted employees to know how to onboard with the company, and employees needed to know the various steps and resources available to them in order to do that successfully.

Here's what we want employees to *feel* in this example: excited to be joining a new company. Engaged with the experience. Comforted and reassured that they made the right choice. And most importantly, invested as a new employee at our company.

These feelings may appear a bit obvious. Of course we want them excited. But how often have we taken the time to create an experience that reinforces that, specifically? Not often.

If narrowing down to the right feelings is a bit awkward for you, start with the opposite instead. In this example, the opposite of what we want employees to feel is questioning their decision, upset, annoyed or frustrated, left hanging, and so on. When exploring the opposite of the desired feelings, you can more easily see the possible friction points and gaps along the way.

This is also why the revised welcome message is much more successful: We have provided *more* details and additional resources, and decreased possible friction points and questions.

Let's continue building out the Employee Experience Framework for Company B. Remember: We are looking at the company-view of what we want the overall experience to be.

Their "Feel"

Unlike defining the Know section, creating an overall Feel can be overwhelming and seem a bit generic. Don't all companies want to be "the best," or "inclusive," or an "industry leader"—and therefore, want their employees to feel the same thing to reinforce these elements? Eh, maybe. In my experience, most companies that say these things don't create work environments or cultures that support that, so we have to dig deeper here.

Company B wanted their employees to feel the following about their company throughout the journey:

- Empowered to make decisions and share new ideas
- Accepted and supported for who they are
- Invested in the company because the company is invested in each of them as individuals

Their Feel list had a few other items, too, but these three are standouts for them.

It's interesting to note they didn't include anything about income-generating solutions. That was intentional. Their company culture firmly believes that employees who feel safe and accepted are more engaged and therefore are higher producers (AKA bringing in more sales). That's why these specific feelings were chosen.

When you look at the Feel section of the framework for your own company, consider the engagement factors of what helps your company be successful and hit your overall company goals. These aren't the captured activities, but instead what motivate and drive your employees to success.

This is the key to knowing you are activating the right feelings across your experience.

Act

The third component of the Employee Experience Framework is Act. Act is where we guide our employees to the next action we want them to take. This is what we want them to actively do—the one next thing.

In some cases, the action can be obvious. It might be something we need them to do right away, such as enrolling in benefits during the annual enrollment period. In other situations, the action needed can be more intrinsic, such as something to learn, keep handy, reference back to, or be engaged with.

Regardless of what we want our journey to communicate at each step on the path, there must always be an action needed. Otherwise, that step is insignificant and increases the chances for confusion and the creation of a friction point.

It's important to weed out "all of the things" we want our employees to do and act upon, and deliver only one action. It's very hard to rewire our processes and communications to reflect one action —but it's important.

Think back to an email you've received from your boss, HR, or your favorite online store.

If we look at Act through the storytelling lens, this is the result or the happy ending along their journey—their success moment. Our hero has gone through an entire journey to meet this one goal—their own happily ever after. This goal is the Act we are creating.

Act in Action

Using the same onboarding welcome message as in the previous two steps, it's clear what fits into the Know and Feel categories, but how clearly does Act stand out?

Typically, the Act can be easily parsed out because it comes with a direct and clear statement to do one thing, known as a call to action (CTA), now. CTAs are critically important to the Employee Experience Framework, as they're the quickest way for us to ensure our employees are following our one needed Act.

With that in mind, the Act in this message does have a clear CTA, but because there is also a lot of other information within this message, the CTA could easily get lost. The Act here is "visit the learning portal to complete onboarding training." That is the one next step we need our employee to take at this stage.

This CTA is stated twice within the message because this message is also an update to welcome and reassure our employees. We have a lot of information in this message, but we are asking our employee to do just *one thing*. We aren't asking them to make more than one choice.

Because there isn't one simple call to action—a direct statement asking the employee to do one thing right now (e.g., click this one button/link)—you have to do a little bit more work to find the Act. We're using this example because it isn't as clear as most of the touchpoints we create—and it shows how you can deliver one CTA while also delivering information without confusing the one next action we want our employee to take.

Let's continue building out the Employee Experience Framework for Company B. Remember: We are looking at the company view of what we want the overall experience to be.

Their "Act"

Creating one call to action is a lot easier when you have a clearly defined action step needed. However, when we look at the overall journey for Company B, it's a bit more difficult to define what they want their employees to do as one action item—as their Act statement.

Company B started to create their Act statement by considering their Know and Feel and coming up with some actions that reinforce those steps. What action would employees need to do and model to make the journey true and move forward in a consistent manner?

Their Act statement is:

> Our employees are invested in growing their career alongside
> our company. They will participate in ongoing learning and
> development opportunities, completing a minimum of two
> growth courses per year.

This Act statement is very closely aligned with Company B's overall journey elements, and it is one call to action (even if it is broad).

You may be scratching your head thinking, "That's great, but our company doesn't have that kind of goal," or perhaps "We aren't a people-first company, so I'm a bit lost." I hear you—and that's often the case. To create to your own Act statement if there isn't a clear overall alignment, consider what the employees are there to deliver for the company. How do your employees' actions add value to your company's overarching goals?

Maybe your statement becomes one of these:

- Our employees deliver value in their area of expertise to ensure the launch of our new product.
- Our employees provide best-in-class service to our customers in their individual roles.
- Our employees manage costs through continuous cost savings efforts that are managed at the employee level and are evaluated on a quarterly basis.

These aren't nearly as sexy as Company B's statement. As they aren't capturing something that entices your employee, these statements are more focused on how the employees support the company's success. And if we're honest, that's what they are there to do.

Let's look at one more example—a hypothetical one this time—to help you see the contrast and how you can apply it at your company. We'll use the Goodwill, a nonprofit most of us are familiar with. The Goodwill's Act statement could be something like this: Our employees will build the skills they need to find sustainable jobs outside of our company.

This statement very closely matches their mission—and it's important to note that they want their employees to gain skills while they are with them so that they can move into sustainable jobs in the world.

Not all Act statements are about *keeping* your employees at your company. They are about the one action you want them to take on a continuous basis while they are there.

Touch

The final component of the Employee Experience Framework is Touch. This component is the *how* we actually connect the experience together—the various ways we touch and interact with our employees. This is the tangible piece of the journey. We can point to it specifically and see it in action.

While this is the easiest part of the journey to spot, as it's typically the only element we have historically focused on, it is also the most wide-sweeping element. Over the past 20 years, as HR has grown and changed in what we do and how we do it, we have continued to grow our touchpoints without much coordination and alignment, leaving us with so many different ways our employees interact with the company.

In order for our employees to feel connected, we have to make sure that the various ways they interact and Touch our company, leaders, and each other is consistent and aligned with our overall goals. To do that, we need to dive deep into creating a touchpoint roadmap.

The roadmap is where we go from the high-level thought process of creating the journey, to outlining the various elements that create the journey—one by one. The roadmap encompasses an inventory of all of the systems, messages, interactions, shared services, platforms, and so on, that employees interact with throughout their employee lifecycle.

If we do a great job at the previous Know, Act, and Feel, but completely ignore Touch, our employee experience will not be changed. This is the most critical component to create true change.

Fair warning: This is the part that we tend to really enjoy because of how tangible it is, but it's also the part that can get very overwhelming very quickly. As you dig into the touchpoints and details, you will uncover *so many* different touchpoints—some of which you weren't necessarily aware of and others that haven't been updated in years.

The gut reaction to feeling this overwhelmed is to add *another* touchpoint or system to fix it all. Frankly, that's the exact reason you ended up in your current situation with so many systems, tools, processes, friction points, gaps, and so on. You've likely already seen this happen in your organization. (PeopleSoft or then Workday implementations, anyone?)

To use Touch appropriately, you may need to add some new systems and tools, you may need to eliminate some systems and tools, and you may need to ditch the various HR systems, processes, and tools altogether. The point is, to be successful in shaping the Employee Experience Framework, each touchpoint is intentionally chosen and implemented to be the best solution right now and then continuously evaluate how well it's working.

Touch in Action

Using the same onboarding welcome message in the previous three steps, let's break down where Touch comes into play. When we are looking for the touch components, we are looking for the actual touchpoints that our employees interact with.

For this message, we have the following touch elements:

- System set-up process (the time line to get login details and access)
- Help desk email address
- Online learning portal
- Manager onboarding plan
- Feedback email address

This one message contains five different Touch elements—and that is only capturing first Touch, not all of the steps, systems, and processes that will be part of the experience once they interact with the first item. For example, one Touch element that isn't explicitly mentioned here, but that we know plays a big role in the new employee onboarding process, is the payroll system. That is its own email but could be something that is included on the manager's onboarding plan. Other items from the manager onboarding email, such as goal-setting, would be secondary elements through the online performance management system.

In action, this can feel overwhelming very fast—almost like you're opening Pandora's box. The key here is to stick with first Touch elements to outline those connections, before you dive into the secondary elements. Basically, tackle first Touch and, when everything at first Touch is clearly captured, *then* dig into secondary elements—and do so in a straight line. In this instance, you would outline all of the secondary touch elements for the system set-up process in-depth, before moving on to capture the help desk, then the learning portal, and so on.

The good news here is that we are likely familiar with most of these touchpoints, either because we own them in HR or because we've interacted with them at some point along our own employee journey. Remember: When we're looking at Touch elements, it's not to solve for them; we'll tackle that later. For now, we want to be able to identify them as elements in our framework.

Let's continue building out the Employee Experience Framework for Company B. Remember that we are looking at the company-view of what we want the overall experience to be. When we examine the Touch element at a company level, it can be the most difficult element to outline because there are just *so many* touchpoints. It can take some time to determine the ideal experience.

Their "Touch"

Company B knew that they had too many Touch elements across the board, but they also knew that they had to work with the systems, tools, and processes they already have in place as they work toward their ideal state. They examined their Touch through two lenses: first, what they want their ideal end state to be, and second, what their current touch state is. This also clearly defined their gaps and what elements, at a company level, they needed to work on.

Their Touch statement is (ideal state):

> We want our systems, processes, and tools—all of our
> employee touchpoints—to mesh seamlessly with our
> employee's everyday lives. Our touch elements will be clearly
> defined, easy to access, and as streamlined as possible without
> losing functionality. We will continue to invest, at a minimum,
> 2% of our profits, into upgrading, enhancing, and supporting
> our touch elements annually.

Their Touch statement is (current state):

> We have many systems, processes, and tools that are confusing
> and hard to decipher for our employees. Also, it's difficult for
> us to support the various tools with expertise, as some have
> such small scope. We haven't been investing in the right
> technology, just upgrading or fixing things when they break
> versus intentional investments.

Their ideal Touch statement really is a statement. What they want their Touch elements to be and how they are going to keep their focus on them are clear. At the same time, because it is such a high-level view of the journey, the details aren't exactly baked in, making the statement feel slightly woo-woo.

That's okay. We are outlining what we want our Employee Experience Journey to feel like for our employees, so we are reaching for "perfection" in the ideal state. At the same time, our company-level statements are our starting point to define the specifics. There will be plenty of time to add the details.

When comparing Company B's ideal state to their current state, they are aiming to decrease the total number of touchpoints, leverage systems fully, and integrate access and usage for all employees. The comparison helps define the gaps, and what the focus should be to be successful. This then leads to the various steps and actions needed to go from the current state to the future state.

A note of consideration: Company B is strongly focused on their people as the key to their organizational success. Their commitment on each part of the journey is all about investing and improving things for their employees, as engaged employees drive their success. However, it's important to note that not all companies do, or should, have the same focus. When you evaluate this section, your company may not want a one-system solution or to invest in their technology annually or streamline the process.

Here's another example of a Touch statement from a company that has a different focus. Their main focuses are serving their clients and delivering profit to their shareholders. There is not a focus or investment on their people as a whole, including investing around engagement, enhancing total rewards, and so forth.

Their Touch statement is:

> Have a clearly defined Touch process with applicable systems, processes, and tools that ensures employees know where to go to access the right element. Our Touch elements will be off-the-shelf solutions that will be analyzed every two years to ensure they are still meeting our needs. Elements will be combined only if there are cost-savings associated with doing so. Support will be provided by a third-party offshore support team, provided by each vendor.

This statement is quite different from Company B's statement. Know that both approaches can work within an organization. To be successful, your journey statements need to support and match up with your company's true culture and goals—not comprised of what you *want* your company to be.

Each component of the Employee Experience Framework—Know, Feel, Act, Touch—builds upon each other as you create and define the ideal experience for your employees, with the goal of engagement and retention. The first component, Know, helps you define specifically what your employees need to know and what they need. By doing so, you're able to be clear in the information provided without confusion or extra fluff. The information is focused and direct—communicated directly based on what will drive their knowledge as the hero.

The second component, Feel, keeps your experience connected by an emotion or feeling, creating the desired mood for your experience. This ensures that we communicate with purpose and that your employees' expected feeling is matched by your own.

The third component, Act, is narrow and defined by the one thing or action your employee needs to take to be successful. It's important that your Act has purpose and that you've guided your employees to the action, so all they need to do is complete it.

And finally, Touch. Our touchpoints need to combine together seamlessly to create the ideal employee experience and reinforce our overall goals. In the ideal state, your touchpoints should be a part of the process that adds delight or isn't noticed. Friction points, bad experiences, or complicated interactions will only detract from the experience, while we aim to blend in or enhance the experience with touch.

6

WHY THE EMPLOYEE EXPERIENCE IS IMPORTANT

We've all experienced what it's like to join a company—and the full range of emotions that come with a new experience. Having been a job-hopper for most of my adult life, I have more stories than most to share. Each experience has been different, and has imprinted a very specific memory and set the tone for my tenure at that company.

Somewhat early in my career, I decided that following my "passion" was more important than having a stable corporate job. I didn't stray that far by today's standards but did leave a good corporate job to take on a freelance assignment while I figured out just what my passion was. And then I stumbled into an opportunity that quite literally changed the trajectory of my career (and life).

While I was freelancing, the CEO of a company reached out to ask if I'd be interested in collaborating with him to create this new department aimed specifically at my skillset and interests. A total dream job basically dropped into my lap! We hammered out the details, and then I was connected with the head of HR to finish the paperwork and confirm the details.

The process went pretty smoothly. She was a phone person, so I was getting several calls each week leading up to my start date, offer paperwork delivered when expected, and everything was ready to go. I was introduced to my new boss in Communications and the rest of the team—ridiculously excited for my start date.

On day one, I arrived and quickly was escorted by the head of HR through security, badging, and new hire orientation. And as she was dropping me off at my new desk—a pod in the Communications department—things started to shift. The warm welcome I was expecting and had been experiencing until that moment, never came. Instead, the Communications team was confused: What was my role, why was I sitting in their department, what was my experience, how was I hired on, and so on? I ended up isolated—not in space, but in collaboration and connection. The team wasn't filled in, I walked into an unknown landmine of a situation, and I had a new boss who didn't know what to do with me (or the new department as a whole).

Suddenly, I went from dream job in my lap to "Wait—what *am* I doing here?" There was a huge disconnect among the CEO, HR, and the department head (and her team). They didn't have a clear process for onboarding someone outside of their standard process, which isn't terrible, but in its absence, they left a lot of angry and confused people in their wake. The department head felt slighted that I wasn't *her* idea (among many other things I'm sure), the new department felt like it was a takeaway from those already at the company, and I felt like I was thrown to the wolves.

In this situation, it wasn't necessarily a process breakdown, but a communication breakdown that took more than a year for me to bridge and fix—and that only happened because I was quickly transferred to another department in the reporting structure. But something as easy as a meeting among the three leaders would have eliminated my awesome-to-awkward experience that left a lasting impact on my feelings about the company.

I share this story because it's so common across many companies. We spend so much time and effort finding the right talent, but then we drop the ball after we've snagged them. While that's bad enough, the part that is detrimental and often overlooked is the way your employee *feels* about your company when this happens.

In my case, I went from extremely stoked . . . to less than impressed and concerned. I then found myself in the position of *apologizing* for the process and constantly justifying my role and over-communicating to try to avoid a similar situation in the future.

There is nothing engaging about this type of experience, and I was forever impacted and influenced by it. They had already lost me when it came to the employee engagement survey. And since I was a leader of a decent-sized team, how would watching my experience influence my team members?

Creating True Engagement

The idea of employee engagement is important and serves as a significant game-changer in our work environments. But with all of our focus on engagement, we haven't done a good job of defining what engagement actually means, as well as how to create it in an ongoing way.

Asking employees about their varying degrees of engagement is fine, but 20 or so years in, we've already addressed the glaring engagement issues. Now we're left with results that aren't necessarily accurate or complete because our employees don't care or don't trust us to deliver anything new—coupled with a shifting workforce who is happy to jump to the next best thing if they aren't feeling the love.

Dang those Millennials! It's not their fault. They are an easy target because we don't want to acknowledge why our engagement surveys are no longer working the way we want them to: because surveys and hokey action plans don't create true engagement.

True engagement comes when you build a meaningful relationship between each employee and the company.

Consider my onboarding experience. What kind of relationship did the company create between them and me? Was it one that reinforced the tenants of engagement? Or did it diminish my relationship with the company?

My impression of the company was significantly dinged. On day one, the company had a lot to make up for in my mind. We were already bickering, without either of us knowing it. This impression not only impacted my onboarding experience, but it also felt like love was lost much quicker when something went wrong over time.

- I couldn't update my mailing address in the payroll system. *"We are a technology company. This is ridiculous!"*
- I needed to open a performance improvement plan (PIP) with an employee and couldn't figure out how. *"Is this a joke? Who is my HR rep? What, she was laid off? Ugh. Is there an ER number? No. Okay, what am I supposed to do to manage performance and why am I wasting my time on this?"*
- Another new corporate decision was made: You can't use your corporate card for travel except to book your flight; we're changing our job titles and band levels; our incentive plan is going to work differently this year; we are no longer going to support working from home. . . .

Whatever the new initiative was, instead of my being able to immediately see the enhancement for the company and for my role, I was annoyed. I questioned why they were constantly trying to make the process *worse*. I asked several times, "Is the company *trying* to lose all of their key talent?"

Every little interaction with a company influences each employee's experience. Without a thoughtful and/or smooth experience, there is *no way* to create engaged employees.

Engagement can only happen when your employees feel as though their company cares and is invested in them as people; true engagement is comprised of the elements in the Employee Experience Framework.

Let's put you at the center of this question for a minute. When you look at your friends, why do you stay engaged with them? What happens when they forget to text you back? Or flake out on a meetup? Or help you move? Or make you laugh?

You stay connected with your friends because you have a relationship with them. And sometimes that relationship gets dinged but other times it gets filled back up—because there are trust and connection.

Your employees' relationship with your company (and remember, you are an employee, too) is built the same way. Employee engagement is not "a thing"; it's the result of having your ideal employee experience in place.

And just like your real-life relationships do, your relationship with your employer is continually changing. You build and break connection over time. With each interaction, each positive and negative experience, your relationship with your employer changes.

Knowing that a meaningful connection is key for building true engagement, we have to focus our efforts in HR and as leaders at a higher level. It's not enough to put an action item in place or to solve for a low survey result score and walk away. These things are great action items along the experience journey, but they aren't necessarily building a better relationship *over time*.

To build a meaningful relationship with our employees over time, we can't only focus on the so-called low-hanging fruit or "1,001 Ways to Engage Your Employees." We have to set a baseline, create points to touch base and check in, open two-way dialogue, and realize that each employee is different (and their engagement factors will be different as well). It's a constant cycle of implementing, asking for feedback, repeating our activities, and checking in—throughout the employee lifecycle.

HOW "EMPLOYEE ENGAGEMENT" LET US DOWN

DURING THE LAST 25 YEARS OF HR, ONE OF THE BIG ASPECTS HAS been, and continues to be that Human Resources wants "a seat at the table," meaning their leaders are getting invited to major decision-making meetings with a revenue focus. Traditionally, HR leaders are *not* invited to such meetings, because oftentimes the more senior, **bottom-line-focused executives *do not* think of them as people who add monetary value to the business.**

Luckily for all of us, this is starting to evolve. You're seeing it change at more in forward-thinking places such as Silicon Valley, but smaller, upstart companies are coming to scale with HR periodically in one of those "seats at the table."

But now there's another problem: **People who are interested in, and came up through HR, traditionally don't have as strong of a business background.** They may understand how to balance a budget, but they tend to not be as strong with fiscal responsibility to the business (and Board), nor know how to prove their value.

As someone who has their MBA in an HR-focused program and after comparing notes with someone who did a different graduate program focused on HR at a top-three school, graduate learning for

HR *still* isn't focused on the right things. If we were asked to focus on revenue plays, compound growth, or even statistics and data analysis, everyone would break out in hives.

My point: Often HR people aren't thinking along the same lines of, or using the same vocabulary as, more conventional business leaders or leaders in different departments.

According to a 2015 SHRM study (the most recent research I could find), there was a 7% *drop*[8] in how other executives viewed the role of HR in their companies. Even as more HR departments want that "seat at the table," it seems as though HR's reputation is moving in the wrong direction.

Part of the problem continues to come back to this: **When HR finally get their "seat," what value can they add?** What should their leaders be doing first to retain said seat?

Getting to the table isn't so hard these days—not like it was 25 years ago. But once you get to the table, stop seeing it as a special achievement or something you should be forever grateful for.

HR deserves to be part of leading company strategy. Don't let the lack of historical participation ruin your effectiveness in the room. HR *may* have a reputation for trying to be people pleasers or non-confrontational or, worse, the quiet/silent types. Don't keep perpetuating this stereotype when you're in the room.

Be the strategic leader you are. Show your fellow departments and colleagues just how valuable HR is—then deliver results.

H(R)evolution

We know that engagement hasn't been working. So what did we do? We pivoted to the next big "HR Transformation." And how does this "transformation" work with employee experience?

To start, it's about changing how HR does work. Mainly by Centers of Excellence (COEs) that separate different HR functions and specialties into different departments.

I remember first hearing about the COE concept, likely on a

Corporate Executive Board for Human Resources (an information subscription hub for corporations) webinar presentation, in the mid-2000s, and shortly after every company slowly started radically changing the way they "do" HR. They made significant investments in new Human Resources Information Software (HRIS) systems (some are already on their second investment in this space), call centers, self-service processing, and so on.

For most companies, the changeover was rocky—regardless of how much (or little) change management was involved. At the end of the day, the way employees would interact with HR was drastically changed from how it was the day before the flip was switched.

HR people were ecstatic (those who weren't laid off as part of the process; unfortunately, many were): They would finally be able to deliver "strategic" HR value and stop doing the transactional work. Except things didn't change all that much.

And now HR people and the employees they partner with are . . . pissed? Bitter? In other words, it's unclear if the big "transformation" worked as well as it was touted. Now we're hearing all about how it's not an HR Transformation, but it's now an "HR Disruption."

But is it?

Don't get me wrong: I love disruption. If you talked to any of my former HR colleagues, they would tell you I disrupted the heck out of their departments when I worked there.

But the next phase of HR isn't disruption. It's an H(R)evolution—and the employee experience is a huge part of how we can get this *right*.

Disruption means the disturbance or problems that interrupt an event, activity, or process. Changing our broken HR departments can't result in having additional problems and disturbances.

We've already provided more than enough of those in the past few years through the first transformation. I understand that the intent behind this new wave is to get HR professionals (and thereby departments) to stop thinking in the same old HR box—to break out of what they typically do and do something different.

But disruption in the workplace is *not* going to earn HR any favors or positive influence at the company. We cannot lose additional credibility in what we do.

And that's why it's time to start the H(R)evolution with the employee experience at the core of your approach.

Here's what I know for sure—not because I've been sitting back and writing *about* the HR space for the past however many years, but because I have been working *in* HR at various companies across the U.S. I've seen the current state of HR, including the knowledge of our HR professionals, the ways our departments are set up, what our leaders think of us, how rollouts have actually gone, and what our employees are desperately seeking.

With the way we are going about being HR professionals, we are quickly working ourselves out of a job/career/profession/passion. Consider that for a moment: We are setting ourselves up for our own demise. For the vast majority of us, while we're sitting at the table, we are not adding significant incremental value. Our leaders are not pleased, and they are definitely not impressed.

And your CEO is about to realize that HR has been holding back. That *you* haven't been delivering everything that is possible because you've been so mired in the "transformation" or the everyday busywork of being in HR. That you've lost the core value *of* HR.

It's not inevitable. It's not something that we can't change—yet. But a new direction forward is absolutely necessary, and it needs to start now.

Fundamental Difference

Fundamentally, we need to evolve past employee engagement and stop labeling the next thing as a transformation. At the core, we must accept that **engaged employees are an outcome of a positive employee experience.**

This is the evolution—the transformation. In the past 30 years, according to Gallup, our employee engagement rate has only gone up by four points. *Four points?!* The average engagement rate in the U.S. is 34, with a 65 being identified by Gallup as Rockstar level of engagement.

We are failing our employees—because we keep trying to focus on the next best and brightest "thing" our industry is telling us. Doing that will continue to deliver the same level of "success" and lack of movement. More importantly, our employees will continue to job hop, be unhappy, and decrease our productivity and profit.

Instead, let's shift and evolve, using what we know to be true, as we all experience it ourselves daily, and focus our efforts there—on the experience.

8

THE FUTURE OF HR

HR IS A RELATIVELY YOUNG DEPARTMENT THAT HAS ALREADY EVOLVED several times over just the past 25 years, so how can we accurately predict the future of HR? Perhaps instead of focusing on what we *think* may be coming, let's focus on what we *know* is true.

The role HR can play has unlimited opportunity for strategic thought and delivery—all focused on an ever-changing work landscape, differing generational needs and expectations, and a more connected world than ever. The C-suite is continuing to look to HR to weed out the tactical and implement strategic solutions.

We no longer can be the department where talent and great ideas go to die (nor do we *want* to be, right?). Or the people who are ignored in the hallway because we are evil.

We are the precipice of a shift in our daily work that is equal parts scary and exciting. Enter artificial intelligence (AI) and see how it's already changing HR in a significant way.

First, I am not an AI expert, nor do I want to be. Second, I think being scared of AI today (at least in HR) isn't the right focus. Third, I think AI is exactly what HR needs to deliver strategic value.

For many people who have been in HR for more than 15 years, this is scary, and you may be resistant to this change—selfishly so, because you don't want to be laid off due to a robot taking your job. I get it: You need a paycheck, you're good at your job, yada yada.

Being resistant to the rise of AI in your workplace is futile. It's happening, and it will continue to become more efficient, sophisticated, and important over time. It's a huge open door that I invite you to walk through with me.

With AI, HR has the opportunity to drop the busywork—the tactical "things," the remnants of personnel—and focus on delivery great strategic HR work without any of the extra clutter getting in the way. Of course, that means that if you're comfortable in your HR role, you may be hesitant to shift your focus and learn a new skill.

But what are your options? If you don't start shifting your skill set from tactical things that *will* be replaced by AI, then you will not have a job at all. Why not use this time gap now—before full AI integration —to become better at your job? More strategic. More focused on delivering the results and high-touch solutions that a robot can't provide.

It's uncomfortable and it takes time to become an expert in a new skill, but it will save you time in your daily work and it will save your job—especially if you focus on the *right* skills for the future.

Using the employee experience as your framework and overall strategic focus is the right skill to focus on, because you are concentrating on how to create more engaged employees (the outcome of the experience), creating an ongoing conversation, and measuring what's working and what's not working (HR metrics)—all of which adds up to what your company cares about: more productive employees who deliver more profit (HR as a true business partner).

Let's embrace the future of HR and work so we can be recognized as critical partners to the C-suite and deliver true effective solutions to support our employees across their employee lifecycle—while helping you find deep value and meaning in the work *you* do.

II

THE EXTERNAL EMPLOYEE
EXPERIENCE FRAMEWORK

The employee experience begins with how our company is perceived externally: the story we share about who we are as an employer, including our total rewards, values, "culture"; what our reputation is; and what someone would "get" out of working with us. In order to attract candidates and our future employees, we need to be an employer of choice.

Being an employer of choice does not mean we have to be on one of the many "lists" like the 100 Best Places to Work. We need to be an employer of choice for our ideal candidates—so we can create and showcase what the experience is at our company, and the right people will be interested enough to apply.

Interestingly enough, this is something most companies already do, but it's not intentional and it's not utilized with this purpose in mind. Instead, companies spend a lot of money on external marketing, usually focused on product, and then slap a Careers page on their website, talk about "what it's like to work here," and pay for job postings where we think their ideal candidates hang out.

This has been working to varying degrees over the last 25 years or so. Especially when the economy isn't strong and we're not concerned with finding talent, talent is everywhere.

But when the talent available becomes tighter, when skill sets are changing with a need for advanced skills and knowledge, and when virtual work is ideal, this approach doesn't work nearly as well as we need it to. Don't believe me? Ask a recruiter. They'll tell you that they're managing a crazy number of open requisitions, they aren't getting as many qualified applications as they need to bring in the right candidates, candidates are ghosting them during the interview process *and* after they've accepted an offer, and so on. This is a direct result of us not investing in the external experience and leaving it up to chance and old practices.

Or look at your turnover rates, especially for key talent and tenure length for your younger generations. This will show you the other side of the coin: how our external experience is attracting the *wrong* talent because we're not being intentional about it.

The way we market our products is similar to the way we need to approach the external experience: to ensure our ideal candidates (and customers) are interested in what our company can offer them.

While HR has the ability to influence a part of the external employee experience (and we'll review exactly how) this experience is shaped by many other partners across our company that help shape and define how we want our potential employees, shareholders, and clients to view us.

9

THE CUSTOMER LENS

BEFORE WE BECOME EMPLOYEES, WE HAVE IMPRESSIONS AND OPINIONS about companies—from either firsthand experience, doing some research, or making snap judgments. We can influence two of these things, but for the most part, we are so focused on other things we only look to influence things once they are not trending in the right direction.

Think back to your own last job search. How did you approach it?

I worked as a career coach for several years, and the typical job search goes something like this. First, approach your network to see what pans out. Then, go to an online job board (or several), find roles that are interesting, and apply. Those who follow the "wide net" strategy will apply to any jobs that match their role requirements without much consideration of the company or research until they get to the interview phase. The other group, with a narrow strategy, will view a job posting, then go to the company's website to see if it matches their culture needs, and then apply.

While we could go down the rabbit hole to discuss which approach is best, the point here is that at some point during the job search process, your candidate *will* research your company. Maybe at first it's so they don't bomb during the interview, but eventually they will be making a decision about saying *yes*—based on what's presented in your **external employee experience.**

We need to start viewing our employees as our customers, and that starts with the external experience. When put a customer lens on our employees—by definition, change the way in which we view them—we are able to better serve them, as we do our paying customers.

We know that our sales teams will not continue to close deals if they aren't selling a consistent product in a somewhat consistent manner (not in approach, mind you, but in features and benefits).

We know that our client support teams will not have clients to support if they aren't able to say *yes* more than say *no,* nor if they aren't able to deliver on their promises, meet their deadlines, and meet or exceed the client's expectations.

We know that our marketing teams will not have budgets to keep marketing afloat if they can't show an ROI on their spend.

And yet, in HR, we rely on chance to share our story and experience—especially when we're trying to entice employees to join us.

While having coffee the other day with a mentee, we were discussing this topic. I brought up a recent experience at a large global banking institution. Ironically, I had just recommended the bank to another entrepreneur, and then my experience with them went left. I went into a branch to open a new business account and make a deposit to an existing account. There were no other customers in the bank, and I was told, "I'm sorry, ma'am. You'll need to call and schedule an appointment with one of our bankers to open a new account."

What? I was trying to give them my business and throw money at them (literally!), and I had to go home, make a phone call to schedule a time, and then come back.

No. Instead, I went to my local bank and opened an account. That's not the moral of the story. Instead, I was sharing with my mentee that my perspective and impression of that bank have now changed—

significantly. Not only will I not be recommending them to my friends and colleagues, but I also will *never* consider working there.

You may be thinking this isn't a big deal, it's one company, and it's my problem. Maybe you're even second-guessing whether, if there was a great opportunity for me there, I would still say yes.

But think about your own list or bad company experiences. Big and small, we remember and consider if it's a place we want to work or if we immediately cross it off our list.

Your current clients and customers are your future potential employees. That's even more true if you're a less-known company or locally based. Instead of hoping a job posting will get your ideal candidates in the door, being intentional—even if you don't have a huge budget to do so—will ensure that your efforts actually pay off.

10

KNOW, FEEL, ACT, AND TOUCH— EXTERNALLY

IN PART I, WE REVIEWED HOW IMPORTANT IT IS TO CREATE YOUR macro ("company-level") desired employee experience so you can align all of the details to one common goal supporting the business outcomes. Aligning your external experience to this framework is critical, but to create a strategy and deliver the right tactics, we need to look at this through our specific audience: our external constituents.

The components of the employee experience are the same even if we're applying them differently externally. We're still going to use the Know, Feel, Act, and Touch framework as the guiding principles that we use to create the macro experience.

However, the answers that we have are going to be very different—because our constituents in the external experience is not our internal employees. Instead, our focus shifts slightly to the experience we want to create for our potential candidates, clients, investors, and so forth.

Know

Just like when creating the macro experience, Know asks: What do our employees need to know, and what do they need? At a macro level for your external employee experience, think about what our future employees need to know. (You can replace the word *employees* with *candidates, clients or potential partners, vendors, investors,* and so on.) What this group needs to know and what they need, before they have joined our company, is different from how we would frame the answers for our internal experience.

What do they need to know about us as a company? In some instances, this could be the same thing as our macro intent. In fact, it should always align very nicely. But because we're looking at it from an external lens, it may not match up. Before you've bought in to a company, you are evaluating the available information to understand company-specific culture elements such as what the company values, what they do, who they are, and more. The external slant is a different focus; we're not evaluating the company or weighting the answers in the same way. Instead, we're evaluating it to see if we want to engage.

These high-level Know experiences may be the activities that your current Marketing department is already doing—and likely doing well. External marketing is usually focused on the reasons why someone would want to engage with, purchase from, or invest in your company or product.

As an employee or as a client, this tells the story of who we are.

However, most marketing Know stories are not usually based in reality or fact. There is a lot of spin or ideal world presentation of an experience. When we take back control of the story for these purposes, it can then become truly rooted in what we want that experience to be and how we deliver it.

We're going to use the same question and marketing story, but our answers are going to have that extra layer helping define why someone external to our company would want to engage with us. This is the Know focus.

What do our potential employees or potential clients or potential customers, vendors, suppliers, and investors need from us? This is where we tend to have a gaping hole right now in the experience. We rely on our marketing materials and public persona to be the touchpoint and external soapbox about what we do and how we do it better and different than our competitors.

When our company is being evaluated against another company, and they find exactly what they need from our competitor, they are not going to move forward in exploring what we can provide. This is true for potential candidates, investors, and customers. Engaging with a company occurs when we feel as though we have all of the answers. We need to make an informed decision—and at that point we stop researching and start deciding.

Currently, we're not sharing the employee experience through that lens. The company that provides this audience what they need, will win —because our audience will start engaging with that company. The more information your audience knows, the more confident they become in their own knowledge about the potential experience with your company. Can they access the information easily to make a decision about engaging?

So, what really, do they *need* to know?

They could need to know big things like our financials, our numbers, how the company's performing—all of those things that, again, most companies do fairly well right now. With the smaller things—those things that are more personal and resonate with individuals—we fall short.

If you think about a future candidate, what they really want to know from us and what they need to know is not only what the environment is like, but also what it is like to work there.

What are our benefits? What's the expectation? What is the level of talent? What is it that we actually care about? Are we people first or not? What is our one over-arching goal that we want to focus on in order to drive success, also known as our "Essentialism goal"?

Do our answers align with what that candidate/vendor/investor is seeking for their next role or their collaboration? This is at the core of the second part of Know: Each person is seeking alignment that allows them to be interested and engage.

Right now, we don't share a lot of information about what the employee experience will be once an employee joins the company. Instead we rely on our reputation—perhaps the size of the company, a well-known brand name, or, if it's a company like Google, the cool factor, the perks they provide to their employees, and their competitive pay practices. Most companies don't have that type of name or perks recognition. There is a void of knowledge about what the experience is going to be once engaged, so the future employee starts researching to learn more and seek alignment.

Research usually starts on your external-facing website or "Careers" page. If, from visiting your site, there is a spark of interest and they haven't gleaned all of the Know details they need for alignment, they will turn to external research portals like Glassdoor and LinkedIn. If we do a better job—even a *slightly better* job—at sharing relevant information and details, we can create alignment on a resource we control (our own corporate website).

This isn't as huge of an effort as you may think. Let's be honest: We think that changing content on our corporate website is a total pain filled with a long lead time and lots of red tape from Corporate Communications. You have a great business case to make the right updates. Having more complete information about relevant information about the employee experience that is important to your future employees, and that is transparent, clear, and easy to find, will improve your candidate and new hire results.

Think back to the last time you joined an organization: What types of company-specific benefits, perks, reputation factors, reviews, and so on did you look at? Outside of your pay, the first thing that most people consider is the company's benefits package (so they can get a more comprehensive view of what working at that company is going to actually be). They are seeking out details about your total rewards package and suite of offerings.

For those of us who don't work in the Benefits organization, total rewards are the offerings (benefits, perks, discounts, compensation, etc.) your company has invested in to help attract, retain, and support employees across their employment lifecycle. Total rewards has shifted slightly in the marketplace from a focus of financial offerings to a total well-being scope. This shift plays into every company's favor— especially companies on the smaller side. Instead of trying to compete on just the financial numbers, you can now provide perks and benefits, at a lower cost to your company, that have a higher perceived value to your future employees.

Most of us are familiar with traditional total reward offerings, such as healthcare benefits (medical, dental, vision). Then you have the more financial offerings such as a 401(k), bonuses, stop purchase programs, and more.

With a well-being focus, you can provide more non-tangible solutions such as discounted gym memberships, discounts on big purchases (such as computers or cars), telecommuting, flexible work schedules, and so on. There's a plethora of different total rewards packages, and each company has their own based on what's important and what they want to invest in. Regardless of what your actual perks and benefits are, this is critical information for our future employees and our vendors and suppliers have.

If what we provide and they *know* about it are lined up with what they are interested in, we are light-years ahead of our employer proposition right now. Our candidates can find what they *need* from us —and they want to engage, apply, and get hired.

That's not the story our external career marketing is presenting right now.

Right now our "Careers" page may have a section saying what it's like to work with us, with a note about how we have these benefits (without any details) or an incomplete description of everything we have to offer—selling candidates short of information that they need and selling us short of sharing all of the perks we have invested in for our employees. Without complete information, our future employees do not have enough details to make a true comparison or an informed decision about why they should choose us. We are losing potential key talent, by not sharing *enough* about who we are and what we care about at this stage in the relationship.

This notion of sharing *more* about our benefits and total rewards, is one that I have gotten some significant pushback about over time. Historically, there has been a lot of hesitation around being transparent and open about the types of total rewards a company offers— especially in a competitive landscape. Companies haven't wanted to share these details because (a) they don't want their competitors to know what is provided and then be *more* competitive by matching and exceeding our offer, or (b) they don't want to lose out on potential talent if their offerings don't match candidates' needs.

Neither of these reasons is beneficial in helping us meet our goal of attracting and retaining key talent—not to mention providing a consistent and effective employee experience. In fact, these reasons are somewhat ridiculous and laughable in today's landscape.

How to Compete

If we are so concerned that our competitors are going to steal our benefits package or share with candidates that we are not as competitive (or more competitive) in certain areas, we are not focused on what we can influence and control. Our competitors have their own set of total rewards that align with their Essentialism goals. They will continue to spend their dollars in a way that best matches those needs —as will we.

We can't influence our competitors' spend, and we shouldn't try. Similarly, many of us feel as though we can't influence how our current company spends their own benefits dollars. We may have some say, but there are certain limitations if we aren't part of the C-suite.

Being worried that our competitors are going to see what we offer and then match or beat us is the wrong conversation and the wrong focus. Instead, we need to focus on what our total rewards differentiators are—and clearly define and highlight these as we communicate our employee experience. These differentiators are the benefits/perks that your company provides that are *more than* competitive—that are better than the market standard or norm. They can be things like the cost of medical insurance. The company may provide extremely low premiums as a differentiator; having many different medical plan options so everyone can find a plan that works best for them; a 401(k) plan that provides a high-match or early vesting; unlimited PTO; no-office/remote workforce; and so on. These are just a few examples; the important thing is finding *your* company's differentiator and leaning in around it.

How? Most of the time you already know what it is. It's that one benefit that seems to stand out. Maybe candidates are always saying something positive about it (or asking if that's really true); maybe it's what attracted you to your company; maybe it's the money-dollar investment or the talking point of your CEO.

Our competitors can copy our benefits as much as they want, but if we have a clearly defined differentiator, then it's not going to have an impact. At the end of the day, what matters to our external constituents —candidates, in this case—is that they are looking for information around the entire suite of total rewards you have to offer.

The same thing can be said about our clients. If they are evaluating two different companies, the lowest-cost provider doesn't always prevail. We all want to evaluate more than just the price. We want to know the value. We want to know the support, and we want to know reputation and information.

This is where the external employee experience needs to be fully on display and transparent, so that we can provide that information to our potential partners before they go searching for it on their own.

Transparency

The second concern is usually around transparency—and the fear we have around repelling the right candidate if we are too transparent. We're worried about knocking ourselves out of the running if there's something really important that our "unicorn key talent candidate" is seeking and we aren't providing.

Here's the hard truth: You may. But stop wasting your time worrying about this. If your potential candidate has a certain set of benefits that is important and critical to them in their stage of life, with their family dynamics, and so forth, by not being transparent early in the process, you are wasting everyone's time.

You're wasting your recruiters' time when it comes to the recruiting and interview stages because, at the end of the day, if that total rewards package doesn't match what that potential employee needs, they are not going to accept your offer. What's worse would be that the candidate accepts your offer, comes into your company, and realizes, whether six months, one year, or two years in, the benefits you offer—your total rewards package—isn't a good "culture fit" for them. Then they leave the company because they have found an organization that provides that one benefit with significant value to them. You're then left without an employee who you just spent so much time, effort, and money on recruiting, onboarding, and training. You are left at square one: finding a new candidate.

Thinking that we can't be transparent about what we offer in a pre-digital and global workplace may have made sense, but now they are hurting a lot more than helping you in the long run.

In order to attract the right partners and future employees, we have to be truthful and transparent about who we are as a company—sharing the information that our prospects need to know about us. The specifics will differ based on your company's own details and really aren't that important. Instead, it's critical to communicate the information in a way that is easily digestible and helpful for your external audience.

Feel

For the external employee experience, we want to approach the Feel section in the same way as we do the macro experience: What feelings do we want an external constituent to have around who we are, what we do, how to engage with us, and so on? This is an interesting component because we're dealing with feelings and emotions—across a more varied population than we are when it comes to the macro internal employee experience.

When we're thinking about how we need people to feel when they engage with our company externally, we usually think about reputational factors. Instead, we want to consider how we want to show what our internal employee experience is like, externally. To do this, we need to ask: What's the warm and fuzzy that we want people to feel, think, and experience when they hear our company name or our company product? We want to evoke a connection, reshaping the way we consider our external reputation/brand, for potential partners.

Sometimes our Marketing group can tell us how our external products and brand should be thought of, but they are from a sales perspective. Our external branding and marketing tend to be focused on creating "buy now" emotions, and not focused on creating a sense of connection or relationship building. Because of this disconnect between what our Marketing team is driving externally (sales), compared to what we want to drive externally (connection), the message is lost for experience purposes. Here are a few examples of external marketing messages that evoke feeling other than "buy now," but are still incomplete experience thoughts:

- Apple wants you to feel cool and unafraid to tackle technology.
- Coca-Cola wants you to feel a little nostalgic and connected to the people around you.
- Nike wants you to just do it, and they'll provide you with cool and trendy shoes and gear to do so.

We want to make sure that, when we examine the employee experience, that our Feel—the feelings we want to create for our audience—matches our true culture experience when our candidates join the company. To do this, we need to decide what the right feeling is and to create an emotional connection to further engage our external audience.

Do we want them to think that we are an industry leader because we are? Or perhaps we want them to feel extremely engaged with our mission?

Let's look at TOMS shoes as an example. TOMS is clear about how they want you to feel about their company—externally and internally. They have clearly defined they want you to feel called and driven to give back to the community. That principle is what led the founders to start the business and what then led them to success. If you're not into that, if you're not thinking about that, if you're not feeling emotionally connected to their mission, then it's not the right place of employment for you. Even if it's a cool place to work, if you don't connect with that feeling, then it is not the right fit.

This level of clarity—this connection to your Feel—is what you should strive for when you craft your external experience. Like the other steps in this process, it *will* help people self-select in *and* out—and that's the goal. We want candidates and external engagement with people who will be successful within our infrastructure, not wasting our time and energy on those who will not become engaged participants in our community.

When determining your external Feel factor, you likely will have a few competing feelings and audiences, all vying to be the winner—especially as most companies are not rooted in the same depth of feeling and purpose as TOMS. However, most companies *do* have a mission statement or core values that can help you get started.

Also remember that most candidates seeking a new role experience a few common emotions when researching their new role: hope, excitement, curiosity, and inclusivity ("fit"). While these emotions can provide a bit of challenge when matching your company culture to your external employee experience, they should absolutely be considered and incorporated into your overall tone and content.

Company B from Part I has a defined macro employee experience for Feel that includes: empowered to make decisions and share new ideas; being accepted and supported for who they are; and invested in the company (mutual investment).

To create our external employee experience, we want to be true to the culture and consider our external audience. Based on these factors, the feeling Company B wants to create for their external audience is self-empowerment. They want their potential candidates to feel as though they are critical components to the company's success, they have the ability to drive ideas and their career with them, and they are encouraged to show up and be who they are every day.

The second part of this Feel step is to take their core feeling (self-empowerment) and ensure that, when they craft their external employee experience and communications, they add in the four common (if applicable) feelings to their tone (empowered, accepted, supported, and invested). They want candidates to feel that the secret to being a contributing member of their workforce is self-empowerment, and they do that by having content written with a focus on *how* inclusivity shows up in their company, excitement around new ideas and where they come from, hope around what's next in the company's time line—and so on.

Their Feel remains specific, but how they express that connects and resonates in a way that is unique to how an external audience wants to engage with Company B.

Being purposeful in your external Feel will evoke the desired emotional connection between your company and your constituents: candidates, stakeholders, partners, and so on. Through the power of emotion, you'll be able to reinforce the important parts of your external marketing messages while also defining what your internal experience feels like—helping you connect with the *right future* constituents to create a long-lasting bond.

Act

When it comes to Act, the external employee experience is applied in the same way as it would be for the macro employee experience: What is the next one action you want your audience to take, to further their engagement and connection with you and your company? While Act can be a bit difficult to define for the macro employee experience, for the external employee experience, this is something that is quite straightforward.

We are creating an external employee experience to help our candidates, investors, clients, and so forth get to know us in a meaningful way—and because we are creating one consistent experience, we are able to define our Act step more clearly based on the audience we are trying to reach.

For job candidates (our future employees), for example, a well-defined Act step will help bring them through our employee experience and direct them to where we want them to go. It will also help us ensure the right candidates continue along in the process (and those who may not be a good fit for our experience culture, opt out).

Let's stay focused on our potential candidates for a minute. When we're thinking about Act for a future candidate, we really want them to know where to apply and what information they need to know about working with us, our culture, our rewards—everything that we hammered out in the Know section—and we need them to act upon it. All of those actions are important and necessary, but we can't ask them to take all of those actions in one fell swoop. We have to create singular calls to action—one small next thing—to help our candidates move through the journey on a well-defined and easy path.

There are many ways our candidates can and should interact with us, especially as they're evaluating whether or not we are the company for them. However, when we give people too many things to do, too many steps, or too many processes, they will leave our site (or sit there frustrated) because the human brain cannot process all these call to actions at the same time.

For most of us, the *first* next action we want our candidates to take is to search for a job and apply. Note: These are two separate actions! To create an effective Act step, if this is our desired outcome, we need to get the right candidates in or self-select out. And it all starts with your "Careers" page, since that's how most companies funnel people into the job search, application, and eventual interview stages.

To be successful at creating actionable steps, evaluate your external employee experience in chunks. From our "Careers" page, we want candidates to search for a job first. We will make it very easy and clear that's what we want them to do. One clearly defined button that directs them to search for a job. We are not going to have people log in first, or fill in various levers or search terms, to get the job search started. One click to bring them to the job search page.

You want candidates to feel like finding the right fit for them is easy and accessible, not that they have to use the right search terms and department designations to find a role. We want *them* to search in a way that makes sense for their own process.

I can't tell you how many times I've gone to a company's website to find a job, only to be frustrated because it wasn't coming up in a job title search or a department category. One role I was hired for was an HR knowledge-based role, but it wasn't categorized in HR. It was categorized in the system under Client Services. I would never have found it unless the recruiter sent me the proper categorization directions.

Our internal job titles, job levels, divisions, job categories, and so on may not make sense to external job searchers. If your Act is to have candidates search for a job, make the process easy and let them do a search on their own terms—not defined for them by your own internal restraints or, worse, those dictated by your Applicant Tracking System (ATS; your online application process or software). Once your candidates are in your search system, you can *then* help them define what they need, how they can find their perfect role, and lead them to your next call to action: apply.

For our next Act, follow the same process—and make this one next step as easy as possible for your external audience.

The default application process for the most popular ATS systems have improved over the years, but for the most part, the experience is atrocious across the board. Consider this: Your candidate has successfully found a role they are excited to apply for and is considering how they will fit in to your company culture—and then they walk away from the process because the application takes 30 minutes to complete.

You *know* this happens frequently if you are looking at your drop-off rates in your ATS. This is unacceptable.

If you have asked a candidate to search for a job, and they did, and now you're asking them to apply, the application process needs to be as easy as possible. What does this mean? It means that they can actually click "Apply" and then apply, without creating an account they may or may not need or without spending 30 minutes filling in every single detail about their work history, desires, skills, references, and more over six pages of "necessary" information. Your candidate is left (a) annoyed, (b) unsure if their time is being used effectively (because, after all, this is just a job application that a computer will evaluate), and (c) feeling like you asked everything short of their medical records.

Your current process probably looks like this, and it needs to change—immediately. I know how important it is to capture all of the work history, details, and information before the hiring stage. But at the online application stage, you are literally nowhere near the offer; you don't need all of these details at this point to determine whether or not the applicant is a viable candidate.

How can you update your external employee experience to be directly applicable and easy, while still capturing the necessary details to evaluate that candidate?

Do you need a resume? Yes. Their legal name? Yes. Anything else? Truly pare down what is needed for you or your AI to determine whether the candidate should move to the human screening pile (or whatever your next step is).

Then that becomes the external application experience. It creates the right feeling and connection, and helps your candidates complete the one Act you need them to do: apply. If you can make it easy and not frustrating, your external employee experience will go a long way in creating good will and surprise for your candidate.

There is nothing worse than spending 30 minutes or more of your life completing an online application in which you rehash your work history, skills, and so on to get an auto-generated email 10 minutes after applying saying you're not a good fit for the role but "we'll keep your resume on file"—thanks to AI. I guarantee you the response to that email is a big "F.U." to the company.

It's important to note that you likely will need to create a separate process once people are in the interview phase to capture all of the legally required information and details for labor laws and offer practices, but you don't need to waste everyone's time capturing this information until the candidate is an *actual applicant.* This isn't a difficult step. It's simply turning on your extremely painful current process once the candidate is in consideration—and maybe improving it a bit so it's not *that* bad.

From here, you want to create the next one action you need your candidates to take in order to engage further with your company. Maybe it's researching your company, or understanding your full suite or total rewards, or watching videos from current employees. Whatever that next action is, focus on that one specific thing and then make it easy for them to complete that action.

The same process should be applied for your other external employee experience constituents. For example, if you are trying to create the employee experience for potential investors, use the Act step to lead them through the most relevant and valued company information to help them make an informed decision about investing. And so on.

Essentially, what you are doing is setting the tone and expectation standards for how our constituents should expect us to create engagement across the various ways in which they want to experience our organization. If we are clear about that and they experience it on the front end, then they will be able to apply that knowledge once they join our organization. They're more inclined to be engaged employees because they are having an ideal positive employee experience.

Touch

The final component of the employee experience is Touch. How touch is applied to your external audience is much more controlled than the macro and/or internal experience. We are still evaluating the various touchpoints our external constituents are interacting with, but luckily the number of touchpoints isn't as endless as it is internally.

The usual touchpoints externally include things like your corporate website, social media accounts, perhaps community activities/presence, and online articles or research websites. Because our touchpoint pool is much smaller than in the internal experience, we have the ability to easily create a more seamless experience externally. Conversely, the population we are speaking to externally is usually more diverse in purpose, covering not just one audience seeking an experience, but instead a wide range of visitors: candidates, investors, vendors, clients, and so on.

When we think about our touchpoints, we want to focus on the ones that we can influence the most, which are typically the same touchpoints we reviewed in the previous three framework components: the "Careers" page on our corporate website. What we want to focus on from a Touch perspective is how things look and feel, the brand, visual interest, content, copy, and accessibility.

Our touchpoints need to be multifaceted—which is not the way most of us currently approach our external-facing touchpoints. Currently, we have a website that is filled with copy (words) and content all about the company written in AP style, with a few images thrown in. Or maybe your company recently updated the website to be more visual, so there are a bunch of images with a little text. Neither version is ideal, nor is it accessible and easy to access on different devices and channels. Depending on the device you use or your own internal information processing preference, the website may leave you disappointed or frustrated. If you like reading text and all you see are pictures, you don't feel like you can capture the information you're looking for. Conversely, if you're a picture person and visit the site on a mobile device, and all you see is a lot of text, you'll be overwhelmed with the content and perhaps be likely leave the site quickly. Instead, we have to consider different accessibilities and learning comprehension preferences when building out communications and touchpoints, to reach the widest audience.

When evaluating your touchpoints externally, be sure to create different ways for your external audience to consume your content. This means using a combination of words and images, but also other things outside of the box, such as video, audio, interactive elements, and so on. We want to be sure our external partner is able to choose their best comprehension mode to better engage with you.

To make the biggest impact on your external employee experience, start with the touchpoint that the majority of your audience will be landing on—their first touch or interaction point. Usually, this is the home page on your external corporate website. After that, they will navigate to the "Careers" page or "About Us" page. One of these pages should be the first touchpoint you want to tackle as far as updating the content and visual identity to match the elements of this framework that you've mapped out so far.

Then, create the different channels or interaction opportunity for different types of info downloads. Add a video, an audio file or podcast, images, a newsletter sign-up, and so on. To do this, you'll essentially repurpose the content and copy you've just updated on the webpage into different and hopefully bite-sized content pieces. To create an audio component, simply read (or hire voice talent) snippets or the entire content of the page and then post the mp3 file. Same thing for video: restate the information in a different channel so you are reaching a wider net of your intended external audience.

Once you have made these updates, apply the same process and steps to your other touchpoints. To ensure you've captured them all, try walking through each step along the way, to see how your company is currently interacting with the external audience. For example, apply for a job and see what happens. What emails do you get? How does a recruiter reach out? How do you schedule a phone screen interview, and so on?

You'll likely find several touchpoints along the way that are completely off brand with what we are trying to create for the employee experience. Perhaps it's a system-generated email thanking candidates for applying. While that alone is bad, the auto-email likely doesn't contain any relevant information or time line details. Maybe another touchpoint is guidance to go to a certain page or video to learn more about the culture, but the link is dead or the content is extremely outdated.

To ensure you're creating a consistent experience externally—especially because we have the ability to influence this a bit more easily—we want to ensure we provide the best first impression for potential candidates and take the extra time to experience as an interested key talent employee will.

This four-component framework to create an effective employee experience is the key to your success at every stage along the employee lifecycle. By using these elements to evaluate and define what the ideal experience is, we can then make the right adjustments—usually small to begin with—and then measure our success along the way. When working on the external employee experience, unlike the macro or internal employee experience, it's important to remember that attracting candidates is not our only goal or outcome. In fact, it's likely not a stated goal for your current employee experience, simply because your external presence needs to serve many other audiences and purposes.

That being said, most likely there is a space somewhere with external-facing collateral to ensure that our story matches and attracts the right candidates and future key talent employees. The good news is that we don't need to spend a lot of money to dramatically change the way our people engage with our company externally, but we do need to be sure we're creating an ideal external experience that matches what an employee would reflect is the ideal internal employee experience.

11

THE CULTURE YOU PRESENT TO THE WORLD

OVER THE PAST 20 YEARS, COMPANIES HAVE BEEN WORKING ON creating their company culture, with an established set of core values, a mission statement, and an overall "feeling" of what it's like for their employees to work there. The problem is that these cultures have typically been created in one of three ways (which we explore shortly), none of which are effective.

When trying to create or establish a company's culture, regardless of the path, they end up having similar issues. A crafted culture is aspirational, top-heavy thinking, and more external-facing than helpful to employees. It's usually cliched or filled with trendy terms, statements, or philosophies—and not reflective of what the everyday employee experience is, which is the true definition of culture.

Paths to Culture

But before we dive into how important employee experience is in influencing a company's culture, let's walk through the different paths to culture creation and why they aren't successful.

Path one: An outside consultant comes in and works with the executives and senior leaders of the company to craft their culture components.

Through implementing the consultant's process or framework, asking some questions, and reviewing the current buzzwords and trends—poof—the culture is "created" and shared with employees.

This path is typical for larger companies (more than 3,500 or so employees) that are looking for an expert to come in fix the situation. A culture rebrand happens when the company is doing extremely well or poor—in other words, when they need something to attract new employees or investors, or to show they are hip and desirable.

This path is very common, and it has, at its bones, the potential to be successful. Hiring an external expert can provide a lot of value to understand where you are in comparison to your competitors and to bring some best practices to the table.

However, this path will ultimately lead to failure 100 out of 100 times. (Note: I should probably say 99 out of 100 times because there is always that one unicorn company that *thinks* they are the exception to the rule.)

Why? Because the approach itself is set up for absolute failure.

Your company's culture needs to be reflective of your actual culture or it will never get any traction internally. And externally, there is nothing to help your culture stand out or for investors or potential candidates to rely on. That's why today, the external-facing culture a company provides is ignored—and why sites like Glassdoor feel more applicable and relevant to candidates in particular.

Another failure point for this approach is the top-down thinking. To believe that your company's executives and senior leaders have any real idea what the daily interactions and culture touchpoints your employees have day in and day out, is laughable. Regardless of how in-touch your senior leaders are, they are still senior leaders.

There is an inherent disproportionate experience between each level of an organization, and culture is rooted in how individual employees feel and interact with a company. Thinking that your culture is experienced the same at all levels for all employees is a huge trap that will create a chasm between what you've stated as your culture and what it is—leading to high attrition and disengaged employees.

Path two: You create your culture in-house by your external-facing experts (Marketing).

Another path to creating your culture is to do it in-house, usually with your external-facing experts in messaging: your Marketing department. This approach is used at companies of all sizes. The intent here is to borrow their experience as employees and the experiences they see on a daily basis, and craft that into a culture statement.

This path tends to have more realistic culture experiences included. However, they still tend to miss the mark because Marketing employees aren't culture experts, the statement can be *too* external-focused, they come to the table with their own biases from being employees, and, while more representative of what employees are experiencing, senior-level input tends to be the focus here, too.

And even if they are great at what they do—creating external-facing marketing messages that influence your external audience—there is still a gap left between what they craft and what the actual culture is, and how other departments can implement and influence these items.

Path three: You copy someone else's culture.

A third option is to see what other companies are doing, whether you're looking at your competitors or following companies that are trendy in the marketplace, and "lift and shift" it to your culture. Most of the time, this path isn't chosen intentionally, but we look to others to help us define our own.

That's not a bad thing in general (unless you're downright copying and pasting; that is always a bad idea), though it doesn't reflect the reality of your culture or your employee experience—which means your external-facing customers, clients, and candidates will have a *very* false sense of what your company is about. It may or may match what they were hoping for, but at the end of the day, they will still be making decisions about your company that are based on falsehoods.

Internally, this approach can cause the greatest amount of friction for your current employees. When you state what your culture is, your employees will try to find those elements in their own experiences. They want to "fit in" and feel connected, especially to your culture.

But if you have copied someone else's culture ideals, your employees are left confused, feeling like they're missing out on something, like they are outsiders, or annoyed that you're painting a picture that doesn't reflect the actual company.

The Culture Solution

If none of these three paths are ideal, how do you present the right culture to the outside world? You start with the employee experience and build from there, using the framework.

We agree that the external culture story needs to match how employees experience the culture in everyday life. Otherwise you risk ruffling the feathers of just about every constituent except for your C-suite, which results in huge expenses: potential lost revenue, shareholders, employees, leaders, key talent, and more.

Unless you are certain (through testing, focus groups, and revisions) that your culture story matches your actual culture, the best path forward is to not present a "culture" to the external world. It may feel like a missed step in the corporate 101 handbook, but let's replace this with something more effective.

First, creating your employee experience journey is critically important and should be your first priority. Because the roadmap spells out what your culture is and can then be applied accordingly, your focus should be there first.

Next, change the conversation about culture—and how you speak about your company—externally. Culture is usually discussed when we're asked questions like "What's it like to work there?" and "What's the culture like?" Candidates might be asked, "What type of culture do you thrive in or prefer to work for?" And investors might be asked, "Does the culture support the growth, numbers, or expansion?"

The word *culture* is a placeholder for different experiences and touchpoints along the journey. It's what we use to prevent us from having to ask the hard questions.

"What's it like to work there? What's the culture like?"

Translation: Do you feel respected, valued, a part of something? Do you have autonomy, or is the norm micromanagement? Do you feel like you can contribute, are your ideas listened to? Is taking vacation respected? Are people supportive or competitive? Can I stop answering emails at a normal time each day, or am I expected to respond in the middle of the night and on weekends?

"What type of culture do you thrive in or prefer to work for?"

Translation: What motivates you? To which type of leader do you respond best? Also, there's something very specific/particular about working in this role; let me tell you about it and see what your thoughts are. Can you work with the leader/team in this role? We need someone who can navigate around or through this specific sticky situation. Are you that person? What do you need to make this job a match?

"Does the culture support the growth, numbers, or expansion?"

Translation: Is the leadership team stable and committed to the path they are currently on? Do they have the right people in the right roles? Is their product for real or just hype? Are employees and leaders heading for burnout soon; is there too much pressure, competition, and/or drama?

Instead of using culture as a placeholder, we instantly create a better conversation—and find out better answers—when we stop using the substitution when we talk about our company.

As an employee or leader sharing your experience, instead of talking about the "culture," talk about what your experience and observations are. Working here is like (fill in the blank). My favorite part of this company is (fill in the blank). My least favorite part is (fill in the blank). (Fill in the blank) is the thing that keeps me showing up every day, and (fill in the blank) are the things that make me roll my eyes.

As a recruiter or hiring manager, it is *critically important* that we change this discussion immediately. I know it goes against so much of the old HR model of how to find talent, but what we're doing isn't working in the long run. Instead, we need to be honest to an uncomfortable point, about what their experience can be like in that role. Present the things that have been difficult for others to deal with in that role in the past, along with what makes it such a great opportunity. Share the reality of what working with their manager and on their team, will look and feel like. By doing so, you will absolutely eliminate candidates and you'll have candidates self-eliminate.

And that can feel frustrating, and you might have a moment of regret thinking that you just let a great candidate slip past you. But here's the truth based on everything we know from the past 30 years: That candidate would have failed in that role and you would be back at square one, trying to recruit for the role again.

The hardest audience to be more transparent about these things is to shareholders. The market rises and falls based on how you present these things to your shareholders—and a lot of time, thought, and consideration need to be put into what you share. Starting with what's true and real, and being honest, is the best route. You will find your fans and investors self-select in and out, based on true factors.

By focusing on the true culture of your company and sharing what the experience is—internally and externally, you will attract the *right* type of candidates, partners, investors, and so on. If you stand behind the "fake culture" you present to the world, you'll create ongoing issues in the long run that will impact your engagement—internally and externally—and create mistrust. Instead, present the true culture to the world, and continue to build, repair, and create your ideal culture and employee experience at the same time.

12

THE CANDIDATE EXPERIENCE

FROM AN HR AND LEADERSHIP PERSPECTIVE, THE BIGGEST opportunity we have with an external audience is how we attract key talent to our company—the candidate experience. Historically, we haven't put much time or effort into creating a cohesive and effective candidate experience. But we've found that in a tight talent market, it's extremely difficult to rely on job postings alone to drive in the right people.

The candidate experience is the first experience our future employees have with our company, and that includes all of the various touchpoints until they start their new role. It's not just about your job-posting software (or boards you've partnered with); that may be how they find you in the first place, but it's just an entry point.

The candidate experience sets the tone for how your employees will feel about your company—from the day they hear about you, until they leave. It is *that* important, and we have been ignoring this to focus on buzzwords like employee engagement instead.

Let me share a story that I've told more than three dozen times across North America to different HR audiences.

I had been out on my own for a few years, oftentimes getting calls about various corporate job opportunities with "offers I couldn't refuse." I am always up for a conversation, but none of the job offers persuaded me that they would be worth giving up the freedom that comes with being a business owner, to step into a corporate job again.

And then a call came from a former consulting client who had a great job opportunity. It had all of the factors that I would need to say *yes*: big team, huge clients, deep work, and so on. I went through the interview process, even flying out for an in-person interview with my potential new boss and some adjacent team members. There were a few bumps along the interview process (mainly untimely responses or lost emails from the recruiter), though nothing that wasn't what we've all become accustomed to as candidates.

The offer finally came, and I was really excited that everything had seemed to come together. I was ready to make the leap back into the corporate world. With the offer came my first surprise: The hiring manager was reorganized into a new role, so one of the other people I met would be my boss. Also, the leader in the group, who wasn't part of the interview process, had resigned.

I thought, "Okay. Not ideal—I was excited to work with her—but I like my new manager, so it should be fine." I accepted the role—and then I didn't hear from the recruiter again.

Nothing. I had no idea if things were confirmed. What to expect on my first day. How I would be introduced to the company, manager, and team. Crickets.

A little bit of doubt starting to sneak in. "Is this typical? Are they excited to have me on board? Do I need to do anything else before I start?" I was still excited, but it was a weird two-week gap of complete silence, leaving me to fill in the blanks. But it was only two weeks, because my first day would be awesome, and I'd hit the ground running.

Day one was . . . interesting. It was a remote role, so I didn't have an office to go into. Instead I sat at my computer waiting to hear more. I didn't have system or email access yet. I didn't have a company phone. I didn't have any directions.

I sat at my desk waiting—and refreshing my personal email, hoping for some direction or an update on what to do and what was expected of me.

I sat there for eight hours and never received a single email or phone call from my new boss, the recruiter, or anyone from the company or team. And for every single one of those 480 minutes, I questioned my decision. My jumping-up-and-down excitement to be starting a new role with so much opportunity, turned into me feeling like I made the biggest mistake of my life.

I kept asking myself, "Do they not want me to start? Did they forget today was my first day? Did I miss an important email or call, providing me with directions? Have I already dropped the ball or failed at some deliverable? What am I supposed to do? Is this how every day will be? Why did I decide to give up my freedom for this? Is this a test?" And so on.

As the day went on, my regret and concern continued to grow until (I hate to admit this part) I was almost in tears with frustration.

This was my first impression of this company after signing my offer letter and becoming an employee, and it shaped the way I felt about the company, throughout my entire tenure. My onboarding experience created fissures in my thoughts about my decision and the opportunity itself. They actively took my excitement and positive outlook and turned it into dread and doubt.

And they were never able to recover in my mind. While I was able to acclimate and get on track quickly in the role, that first day shifted the way I looked at the way the company did everything. I saw the negative of each decision, not any excitement of new possibility.

It wasn't all bad—far from it—but that experience changed my perspective of what was valued at that company.

This is an extreme example of how onboarding can go wrong, but every time I've told this story, I get the same reactions: the same gasps, the same nodding heads, and, in the right audiences, some acknowledgment of their company having a similar hands-off focus on onboarding.

Usually I ask for a show of hands and ask, "How many times have you had a new employee roaming the halls or sitting in the lobby for hours on end on their first day because they don't know where to go?" It's *always* more than half of the people in the room—with several saying *they* were that person.

It's not intentional, and we don't want to create a bad first impression to our candidates who will become our employees, but we aren't focusing on creating a consistent experience. Instead, we're focused on other activities or we let the different groups or systems manage the process, until they become internal employees.

But once our employees have had a certain experience with us, that has a long-lasting impact on their overall relationship with our company—regardless of how many "employee engagement activities" we throw their way. Let's walk through a few ways we can create a better candidate experience using the Employee Experience Framework at each step (Know, Feel, Act, and Touch).

A Note about Candidate Company "Culture" Information

There are general company information and experience factors that are usually referred to as "culture" that candidates will experience at various steps along this process—through their first day as an employee. It's important to remember that many of these touchpoints are not standalone experiences but help dictate the overall macro experience.

These information touchpoints may include things like the total rewards, differentiators, culture, mission statement, values, work environment, leadership philosophy, and more. Throughout this book, these items are explored through the Employee Experience Framework, to help you determine what they are for you company and how they can best support your experience and engagement results. While not necessarily called out as knowledge needs or touchpoints at each stage, they are always in the background making up the macro experience. If what you are creating, communicating, and reinforcing during each step of the process does not align with these larger concepts, you will create immediate friction points and, worse, distrust, thus eliminating any sense of real connection you've worked so hard to create during the process.

This is also why transparency is more important than keeping things like your total rewards package or goals a secret. Your competitors can't replicate your company and employee experience as a whole—even if they know the different components—but they *can* communicate more effectively, if you're not transparent.

Remember this perspective as we dive deeper into various steps along each process below.

Recruiting Process

When a qualified candidate decides to apply for a role at your company, they are making the first move to create a relationship with you. Before online applications, the process was a lot more personal if not more tedious: mailing or hand-delivering a resume and cover letter on special paper, addressed to a specific person, and hoping to open a dialogue. The same is true now, but it's online and filtered through job boards, resume-scanning bots, and buttons to easily sort each candidate's viability.

And the HR market keeps flocking to the hot, new and improved online tracking system that saves recruiters time and the company money—at the expense of your candidates. While these systems are incredibly helpful and a must in today's marketplace, we have been relying on them to manage our candidate experience, and it's leaving a bad impression on our future employees.

When evaluating your recruiting process from an employee experience perspective, you first need to understand what a candidate would need to Know, Feel, Act, and Touch at each stage of the process. For example, when a candidate is at the application stage, they will need to Know, Feel, Act, and Touch details about the application process, versus what a final candidate at the offer acceptance will need to Know, Feel, Act, and Touch. As a candidate moves along the recruiting process, or the employee lifecycle as a whole, the candidate's baseline knowledge and their needs change—and we have to continue to evolve our communications to match each candidate where they are along the process.

And the touchpoints to incorporate, eliminate, or rely on at each stage of the process is vastly different. Right now, if you're using a popular ATS, you haven't considered the different stages that the ATS touches, so it's an off-the-shelf solution and delivery based on what the software can do.

Let's fix that so the experience you're providing attracts the right candidates (making your job even easier) and repels the wrong candidates (saving you time and effort in the long run).

Here are some things to consider along each step of the process, that you can apply right now to your company's own recruiting process.

Who Recruits for You

We need to start at the beginning, with a decision that has likely been made long before you even arrived at your company: Who is responsible for recruiting? Recruiting is one of those skills in HR that often gets overlooked or simplified, especially in a good job market or if you work at a company with a recognized name.

But recruiting well *is* a skill—and understanding clearly where the skill level is, is an important for step.

The most critical skill any recruiter possesses is knowledge about your specific role. Yes, they need to be able to read resumes and interview properly, but they are only able to be effective in their role if they know exactly what they are hiring for first.

This step sounds easy, but when recruiters these days tend to carry more open requisitions (job postings) than manageable, deep knowledge about a role is definitely not at the top of their mind. To help your recruiters succeed, we need to slightly reframe the process on our end, since we're likely not influencing "bad recruiters," the number of postings each recruiter has, training them in your method, and so on.

Using the framework, we're going to help our recruiters find us the right candidates—getting us in front of our current barriers.

Know

When you are ready to open a requisition, there is likely a process: questions you need to answer for approval, a form in which you provide the job description, and so on. Work within the process but provide *better* information.

Instead of simply copying and pasting the corporate job description or the one you used last time, really think through the posting in two lenses:

1. What does the recruiter need to know about this role/team to identify the right candidates when they cross their desk? What are the actual skill sets they will be using daily? What are the "no-go" factors they need to look out for?
2. What do candidates need to know about what they will be responsible for, what a typical day looks like, what the team is like, and what the expectations are?

We cannot keep posting fluffy job descriptions and hoping for people to be inspired by them—and not disappointed when the actual role looks nothing like what we told them it would when they join the company.

Your job description needs to be updated to include these items, as well as be very clear about what their experience will be once they are in the role. This will take some extra time for you to put together (budget 30 minutes or so), but your job description will be more accurate and help candidates self-select more effectively.

Feel

When we are posting a new job opening, we tend to do so much work to get it approved and opened (budgets are tight and you likely worked through a gazillion levels of approvals and justifications) that we are so *over it*. We forget that for our future employee, this is a really exciting time.

The same goes for our recruiters. They are overworked and underappreciated, in general, and to them it's just *another* job posting on their plate that they don't have time for.

We have to create the right feeling and emotion for both audiences, to ensure our job posting has the opportunity to succeed.

We want recruiters to feel optimistic about our role—and optimism comes with knowledge. Remember how I said that the closer they are to role from a knowledge perspective, the easier it is to recruit for? We want to encourage as much optimism and excitement around our role as possible, so we are going to go above and beyond with providing our recruiter the knowledge and support they need for our role.

We do this by providing a Recruiting Brief as part of our requisition. This is a best practice to help your recruiter (or recruiting team) learn as much as possible about what you're looking for, without it being a tedious process. It starts with conversations with your recruiter when they have been assigned your role. During the conversation, you'll want to identify the skills that will be used in the role, knowledge or experience that is necessary or can be learned over time, the type of culture your team has, work environment, expectations, and so on. The conversation allows for both of you to ask and answer questions, to ensure you're sharing relevant details and your recruiter gets the information they need. From there, the best practice continues with a document that you share during the early stages of the recruiting process. This document outlines the details of the role, in some ways recapping your conversation, but also providing a document your recruiter (and you!) can refer to during the recruiting process. It is a template for the role and your best candidate—to continue to use and tweak as you go through the recruiting process.

In the Recruiting Brief, you'll include the expected role details—title, reporting manager, direct reports (if any), budget responsibilities, daily duties, requirements, and so on—and additional details such as:

- Computer programs and knowledge level needed (and if it can be trained to or needs to be at a certain level from day one)
- Client expectations and their culture
- Work hours, work environment and expectations
- Percentage of the type of work daily, weekly, monthly—and the type of thought expected (innovative, entrepreneurial, task, and so on)
- Team dynamics, interactions, communication channels

> *Go to bettHR.com/brief to download the Recruiting Brief template.*

We want candidates to feel excited about our role specifically—and realistic. This is a departure from how job postings are typically created. They are usually boring and filled with words and descriptions that are generic and disconnected with how people experience work. Instead, we are going to be realistic and share actual responsibilities, duties, and expectations to help employees get jazzed if that matches what they're looking for—or not applying if it's not a fit.

We want the job description to *connect and resonate* (in other words, create an emotional reaction) with the applicant. To do that, we have to stop using fluff and ideal state, and instead be realistic and practical with what we have to offer in our role.

Now that we have our feelings mapped out for the recruiter and the applicant, we can consider the actions we want them to take.

Act

At this stage in the process, Act is rather easy to define. We want our recruiters to recruit: post the role, find the best candidates, do some weeding in and out, and get qualified talent to the interview stage. And we want qualified applicants to apply for our role.

This step is so closely tied with what both parties want as part of their drive to work that it is usually a plug-and-play solution. We post the role on our website and applicable job boards, then we wait for candidates to apply, hoping that the AI process eliminates candidates who aren't a match and shares the ones that are.

We want recruiters to recruit and we want applicants to apply at this stage—but we want both to feel valued and connected when taking their respective actions.

And we want to make it as easy as possible for both to take the one next action we need them to take. That means eliminating all possible doubt and friction points along the process, so their only option is to take this next step: recruit or apply.

Touch

The systems and tools that we use during the recruiting process vastly shape the experience that both recruiters and candidates have along the way. A majority of companies use an ATS or other HR software or job boards to help with this process.

There are *so many* issues with the current systems out there (which we aren't going to dive into here) that, as part of our Act evaluation for this step, I recommend you take a quick look at what the system does and says for applicants.

Here's why: If an applicant just took 30 minutes of their life to walk through the lengthy and painful process of answering all of the ridiculous questions your ATS asked them just to have the honor of "applying" for your role, they deserve to be treated appropriately.

For example: Does your system send an auto-generated response five minutes after a candidate applies saying, "Thanks, but you're not qualified?"

I have gotten hundreds of those auto-response emails over my career, and each time my reaction was not great—and I *know* how those systems work. In fact, each time I got one of those emails, I talked back to my inbox saying, "Really? I am *so* qualified for that role. Your loss." And I never applied at that company again.

Candidates who are not right for your role deserve to be treated decently for, at a minimum, investing their time to jump through your company's hoops to express interest in your company.

I'm not saying that an auto-generated response isn't appropriate to use at this stage (when the candidate has only completed an online application), but make sure that the response is kind, reflects the experience you want them to have, **builds** a relationship with a future candidate, and doesn't make the candidate feel like they wasted their time and effort.

Make sure the touchpoints play to your advantage during the recruiting process. Use the right systems/channels for your recruiter to be efficient and start building the right dialogue with your candidates as a whole, regardless whether they are perfect for your role now (or later).

Selection Process

Now that we have qualified candidates, we need to have some conversations and research to see if we are good fit and if they are a good fit—through interviewing.

We have all been interviewed before, as candidates, and most of us can share a really bad interview story or two. And if you're in HR or are a hiring manager, you probably have hundreds to share.

The process of selecting our best candidate through the interviewing process is critically important for the *one person* we want to eventually hire, but it is also a lot of work and coordination. It can feel like we're having to kiss a lot of frogs to find royalty (and it's often true).

This is also where things tend to go *really wrong* for key talent—especially in a good job market.

Your selection process, cadence, responsibilities, and time line need to be figured out and agreed upon before you open your requisition. Full stop.

For the past two years or so, there have been a lot of posts circulating on social media around candidates ghosting, candidates sending "thanks but no thanks" emails, and candidates changing their mind. A lot of these actions can be attributed to the selection process being broken on the company's end—not, *ahem,* because candidates are Millennials, as some have suggested.

If candidates are not nurtured and connected during the selection process—as in, they do not know exactly what to expect and when to expect it by—they will fill in their own story and seek alternative options.

Using the framework, here's how to map out your candidate selection process.

Know

Once your recruiter or you have identified a qualified candidate, you want to take them on the next step of your interview process, whatever that is for your company. With that, you will start the Know exchange with that candidate.

Have an actual timetable with the process defined for each role that you hire so you can deliver knowledge and outline the experience accordingly. Candidates need to know what the process is and the time frame over which it will take place—at each and every step. Your recruiter needs to know when you will be reviewing candidates, interviewing them, and making yes/no decisions at each phase, and when your expected hire date is.

As candidates are being interviewed, they also need to know what the role truly is, what to expect, what you are looking for, and what the deal-breakers are. This is the transparent and honest part of the interview; we have to help candidates know what they are truly seeking out for their next step in their career, before we waste anyone's time.

It's so tempting to fall back into bad habits and go through the selection process the way most of us are now: holding everything so tightly to our chest with the hope of not losing a candidate or making a bad decision. Or maybe it's just a power play? Regardless, the current process is broken. To attract and select key talent, we need to be strategic and thoughtful about how we want our potential employees to experience the selection process, as we have already started building their engagement story.

Go to bettHR.com/selection to download the Selection Process template.

Feel

During the selection process, we want to evoke very specific emotions—and very different emotions—within our recruiters and our candidates. Remember: When we consider the feelings we want to evoke at this step in the process, we are helping to build the right type of relationship to reinforce engagement and a positive interaction.

Recruiters want to feel accomplished and add value in their role. Most recruiters get a real sense of accomplishment and satisfaction when they can make a connection between a candidate and a role. During the selection process, this is the main feeling we want to evoke for this audience. The hiring manager's role here is to provide feedback, information, and updates along the way—helping the recruiter know as much as possible about the role so they can find the perfect match.

For candidates, the selection process needs to provoke a very different emotion: Candidates need to feel excited and optimistic about the role and opportunity.

If we liken finding a job to dating, this phase would be courting. We are trying to explore each other and see if it's a good match, while at the same time hoping it works out. We're eagerly anticipating the next date, uncovering more information, and seeing if we're ready for commitment.

Frankly, most companies are not evoking positive or optimistic emotions during this process. By not being intentional about our employee experience for the selection process, we are creating the opposite and very negative emotions in our candidates. They feel ignored, like one of many in a process—not a top contender/key talent. They are not excited about the company or the role, because they don't want to get their hopes up, so they keep searching and applying for other roles. Basically, they are waiting for a better offer to come along or ghosting you.

Consider the difference in these emotions—what we're currently evoking and what we want to evoke for a potential new employee. Which emotional state will create the best experience and an emotional connection?

If we were dating someone who got back to us when they felt like it, ignored our emails, didn't set our next date until they felt like it (and mind you, weeks may have passed), isn't telling us if they're into us or not (or worse, telling us we're being considered when we're really not), and/or they take no action, we would break up with them in a hot minute.

Your candidates are doing the same. While they may not be withdrawing their candidacy—because hey, people still need to work—they are emotionally disengaged with your company before they even walk through the door.

Act

Similar to the sourcing process, here the action we want our recruiter and candidates to take is quite clear: We want our recruiter to continue to manage the process with our candidates and reinforce the desired emotion, and we want our candidates to continue along the selection process to be ruled in or out.

As we communicate during this stage, we want to be very clear about what that one next thing is. For our recruiter, we need to limit our own urgency to fill the role and, instead, help guide them to the next one thing we need them to focus on (managing the candidates). The easiest ways to do this are with your recruiting time line and your recruiting template with the role details.

For candidates, we want them to stay connected and engaged in our recruiting process (however long and/or painful it may be). To do so, you want to give them specific check-in points or days: details about when they will be hearing from you, what the process is, who will be part of the interview team, and so on. Their one action is to *stay* in the process—the fewer distractions, the better.

The more systemized you can make your selection process, the easier it is for both audiences to take the next desired action.

Touch

The selection process tends to include the most touchpoints for our external audiences. Because of that, there is usually one main system (ATS) that coordinates many of the communications. Outside of that, it can be all over the place. And remember: We've already confirmed that our ATS is not sending great communications as it is.

For recruiters, the touchpoints need to be easy to use and easy to integrate into their workstream on a daily basis. If they need to source with one platform, the ability to review and share resumes, schedule interviews, or reject candidates needs to be part of the sourcing system. The more steps or systems needed for recruiters to efficiently keep to their selection process and plan, the less likely it is that it will be effective—leading to frustration from the recruiter and a lack of communication to the hiring manager and candidates.

For candidates, the various touchpoints, often in conflict, are frustrating but not usually detrimental. They are used to ATS platforms to apply and receive auto-generated emails. Here's the thing, though: A generic "You've been selected to be interviewed" email is a lot less impactful than a message coming from the recruiter with a link to a scheduling app.

Here's what that would look like (and this can be automated):

Hi Candidate,

We're excited to share that we think you may be a great match for XX role at YY company. I'm the recruiter for the role, and I'd like to set up some time to learn more about your experience. Please find a time that works best for you, through this link, in the next five business days. Be sure to provide the best phone number for us to chat live. Looking forward to our interview!

Best,
Recruiter Name

This can still be auto-generated, but it's a lot more personal than "You've been selected." Also, special flashing note to anyone who schedules interviews: We are in the age of online calendars. No one on this planet needs to go back and forth a gazillion times to find the right date/time to chat. Send a calendar link, for the love of Nancy. It allows you to choose available times and options so you can still manage your own calendar, but it also gets you out of the nonsense of coordination.

Note: This may not be ideal for group interviews or if you want to do a series of interviews in a row. But if you're trying to schedule a one-on-one interview of any kind, use an online calendar app.

Email is likely the most frequently used touchpoint at this stage in the process outside of an ATS. To help create a consistent experience and save all parties time, craft various email responses that are typical (e.g., you've been selected, we want you in the next round, you aren't our candidate but thank you, ready to extend an offer, and so on) and save them as email templates. That way, you can still create a consistent experience, but you can personalize it so you're reinforcing the right feeling and helping candidates take the desired action at each step.

A Note about Interviewing

The way we interview a candidate is unique, based on our own experiences and what we think is most important to discover during the selection process. The best way to interview isn't a perfect science, but in general we could all improve our process.

To be more effective while interviewing potential candidates, start with your desired macro employee experience in mind. From there, ensure you are focused on learning more about each candidate in the areas that match the Recruiting Brief you used the framework to develop.

By doing so, your interview will be more closely aligned to what success will look like for both parties. Instead of hiring for a personality that you like, or a great on-paper resume, you will be hiring for a realistic experience fit first—with the candidate's skills and experience taken into account second.

This takes a lot of practice and constantly reminding yourself the true purpose of interviewing: finding the right talent for the right role —not someone who you think will be easy to manage, has the right company names on their resume, went to the best college, you want to hang out with, and so on. Although none of these things are ideal qualities to hire from, it's unrealistic to think we aren't considering them at one point or another. But remember: The more realistic and transparent both parties are during this process, the more likely you are to find a fit that is set up to excel when they start.

Offer to Start Date

Once you've selected your best candidate, it's time to move to the offer stage, which is quickly followed by the new employee's start date. While these are two distinct phases, I've grouped them here because they should flow seamlessly, and the same feelings should be created during this time frame.

The offer process tends to be different depending on your company, but typically it starts with a verbal offer to the person chosen, then there is some negotiation, and then an offer letter is sent for agreement. Oftentimes this process is managed by the recruiter (if you had one) or HR; for hiring managers, it can be a bit of a gaping void of action and information. But you are still a critical part of the process, as it's an extremely important touchpoint on the employee experience journey.

As part of the selection process, you should also be working with the recruiter to map out what the offer to start date process will be, so you can create a consistent experience and agree upon how your chosen candidate will process the offer to start date time frame.

Because most of us don't tend to manage the mechanics of the offer process and will likely have to work within the framework our company has established, we will focus here primarily on the time frame between an accepted offer and the new employee's start date—right before we enter into the onboarding process.

Know

There is usually an extensive amount of information our future employee needs to know at this stage in the process. And since it's broadly the same information regardless of the person's role, title, pay grade, and so forth, you should have a standard process of sharing important information.

Think back to when you accepted an offer and were waiting for your start date. What were your questions (big and small)? What steps did you need to complete to ensure you were ready to start your new role?

Remember: If information is lacking, we fill in the blanks with our stories—which are usually a lot more negative and biased than reality. We need to share the right information at the right time here to reinforce the emotions we created during the selection process.

When sharing information during this time period (typically two weeks), be specific with all of the steps the new employee needs to take, the turnaround time for each action item, a contact person for questions, and so on.

Here are some things to get you started in outlining your own Know at this stage. This list isn't exhaustive, but rather a starting point to help you determine what your candidate may need to know when they receive an offer:

- When is my start date?
- Who is my manager (title/contact information) and how does this role fit into their organization?
- What pre-start testing do I need to complete? And once completed, when will I hear back from you that I've passed that stage?
- What are the details of my employment (title, salary, pay dates, benefits, payroll information I should gather, contracts, bonuses, etc.)?
- What should I expect or plan for, for my first day?
- How and when will I gain IT access (email, systems, a computer, etc.)?
- Who should I reach out to with questions and/or to ensure I'm on track?
- Who is reporting to me (titles, roles, locations, responsibilities at a high level, etc.)?

Feel

Maintaining the right emotions at this stage is critically important to ensure our new employee, when they start, is connecting with us and our company the way we hope they will. This sets the stage for high engagement during their tenure. If we get this wrong or let each future employee determine their own feelings at this stage, we will end up in the same situation we are in now with employee engagement—not ideal.

In general, we want our future employee to be excited, hopeful, and optimistic about joining our company in their new role. We want them to feel like they made the right decision and that we're excited to have them join our team.

Just as we can't actually influence engagement, we can't influence how each person actually interprets and processes emotions—but we can create the best guided experience possible here.

To do this, we want to provide moments and experiences to reinforce these emotions and take advantage of each communication (verbal, electronic, etc.) to capitalize on building the desired emotional connection. These are little things and big things—and all can be incorporated into your process, to reinforce the experience with a little foresight.

At this point in time, the person is still external to our company. They're on their way to onboarding and joining our team, but until they arrive on day one, we should still look at this through an external lens.

Here are some ideas to consider when incorporating Feel into this stage:

- Have a cadenced communication schedule to keep in touch with the future employee so they feel connected and in the loop. Maybe it's every three or four days during this time period—whatever you think works best. With each outreach, remind them how excited you are to have them joining your team.

- Send them information about the company and team that is external-focused to remind them why they chose you. This can be a recruiting brochure or highlights of what you may share when pitching new business. The goal here is to foster the excitement of all the great things going on at the company they are about to join.
- Create a time line PDF so they have all of the details they need when they sign their offer letter (what to expect when and the various time expectations).
- Share a bio of their manager, or make it more comprehensive to include fun details/bios about the team, like an early "get to know you" document or interactive experience.
- Snail-mail a welcome package or card. This can overlap with the onboarding process, but at this stage, it would be focused on welcoming your new employee and helping build excitement and a sense of belonging.

Be sure to leverage every interaction and opportunity to build excitement and reinforce the emotions you want your future new employee to feel as they are about to join your team.

Act

All of the time between the offer and your future employee's start date, is about one action: them showing up for work on day one. It sounds like this action doesn't need to be defined or mentioned because the candidate accepted the offer letter and, in theory, wants the job.

But if you've had to hire an employee in a tight talent market combined with the current job practices and generational norms, you know about the trend of potential employees ghosting on their first day. They simply never show up, sometimes without any reason, and you're left without a new employee to onboard.

So, the action is clear: make your offer (which they already accepted, mind you) so irresistible they can't resist.

When you keep this at the forefront of the next one thing, combined with being clear about the knowledge they need to know, the feelings you want to evoke and eventually how they experience the various touchpoints, you are reinforcing the desired action and outcome.

Touch

Your future employee is still in between being an external candidate and an internal employee, so the touchpoints they experience, particularly during this "dead space" between offer acceptance and start date, will likely contain many variables that you can't control or influence. These are the company-mandated things that can include background checks, drug testing, IT/systems setup, payroll, and more.

When evaluating the various touchpoints, instead of trying to pare them down or leverage them all correctly like we would at most other stages, at this point in time the best approach is to let Touch be secondary and ensure you over-deliver on the knowledge they need to know.

If you're clear on the various steps, touchpoints, systems, and so forth up-front, along with what they are for; the time line; and how and when to access them, then the touchpoints become a series of interconnected action items—not confusing systems that your future employee needs to learn and spend effort figuring out.

Remember: This stage is focused on getting your future employee to walk through the door on day one, which is when they officially transition to an employee—and your focus shifts to onboarding and their internal employee experience.

For most companies, the current external employee experience has been focused on one page of the company's website: "Careers," if it has even been intentionally designed. Then, when your external constituents interact with the information that your company has available, they are knee-deep in marketing and sales communications, which present the absolute best or ideal state of the company forward. This leaves your external constituents—candidates for employment especially—with an inaccurate or incomplete impression.

This leads to a huge shock when your candidate becomes an internal employee on their first day of work. They created their own story, expectations, hopes, dreams, goals, and pathways to success for their new job, and then quickly realize they were missing significant details of the culture story. That's why the external experience is so important: It primes your future *internal* employees for a successful transition into your company. With that, your previous external candidates as they become new employees will be able to better match their own expectations and pathways to success with what your company needs from them, from day one.

III

THE INTERNAL EMPLOYEE EXPERIENCE

By definition, the employee experience is rooted in how internal employees experience your company. Historically, the focus has been about engaging them, treating them like humans, or having them buy in to our culture while they're working at our company, if our company has even considered this at all.

As the workforce and expectations continue to change, we know that the employee experience is more than what takes place once we've onboarded an employee—and it's much more than engagement activities, human-first thinking, and an ambiguous culture.

This section is about how to create an effective employee experience for your employees, once they have joined your organization. You've already convinced them that they want to be a part of your team—and they decide that on a daily basis when they show up. Now it's about how to deliver on your promise and keep them excited about *being* on your team.

It's the meat and potatoes of employee engagement work (and probably what you thought this whole book would be about!). Ready to create an impact on your employees and deliver real results? Let's get started.

13

INTERNAL PERSPECTIVE AND LENS

BEFORE EMPLOYEES JOIN OUR ORGANIZATION, WE SPEAK TO THEM through the customer lens: sharing the experience from an outsider's perspective with transparency and truth (with a little marketing and sales language thrown in). But once a candidate becomes an employee, whether starting today or 10 years ago, our responsibility shifts greatly. No longer do we think of them as external constituents, but as internal team members.

Here's the thing, though: Your people are your greatest advantage, not your product or service. And while it's important to focus on the external things you do to generate income, it can't be at the expense of the people who are standing with you (your employees). This shift in consideration is usually not intentional, but it is ingrained.

If you look back to the various ways our workforce has developed, beginning with the Industrial Revolution, to mass production, to women entering the workforce, to today's digital workforce (which is changing by the moment), the role employees have played has changed as well. The ideas of "every employee is replaceable" and employees being simply "cogs in a machine" are still prevalent—when the reality of those statements couldn't be further from the truth.

Yes, people are easily slot-able into *certain* roles at varying degrees of success and competence, but the premise behind this idea is false for today's work. This is a company-first perspective that relies on employees to deliver the desired outcomes without any care or investment in employees as individuals. There are still *many* companies out there that believe in this culture-focus, with varying degrees of success—and even lower degrees of key talent in their ranks. In other words, their lack of investment in their people attracts the *wrong* people for efficiency, innovation, long-term success, and more, which results in companies spending more money, not less. And that's without taking the sunk onboarding costs into account.

A slight shift can resolve many of these issues, without the company changing their core mission and stakeholder responsibilities. That shift is to look at and treat their employees like they do their customers. Most companies know how to build a set of standards and expectations around customer experience and relations. Or, by default, they go by the "the customer is always right" concept. The key here is to look at your employees as constituents that the company serves, not just cogs in the wheel.

Note: This approach is much different than being a people-first culture (more on this concept in a moment). This shift creates an employee-focused mindset or customer cohort that we serve. What our company believes in—from an employee, total rewards, investment, and so forth—doesn't change with this shift. What *does* change is the conversation around those who are responsible for delivering the work for your company.

Instead of employees working for your company, they are working *with* your company to deliver results. They are a part of the chain of delivery to achieve your company goals and profits. Your "cogs" are built by individuals who are invested in (engaged with) the outcome because they feel valued for the unique skills they show up with every day. We then are able to create best-in-class experiences for our employees, just like we would for our external customers.

A Note about People-First Cultures

For the past five to 10 years, incorporating the idea of being a "people-first" culture has spread like a wildfire throughout company mission statements and values, incorporating sentiments like these:

- We put our people first.
- We care about our employees.
- We are committed to providing a good company culture.

Then it became a trend. In today's digital workplace and with younger generations saying they want to feel valued and connected to their work (above anything else), *saying* you are a people-first culture helps attract these audiences and gain external favor.

The problem is, not all companies *are* people-first. And that's okay. The problem comes when a company says they are people-first and they aren't.

There is some shame or embarrassment (and a lot of cringing), particularly among HR professionals, about the people-first concept—especially when they know that their company is not a people-first company. I've had HR people ask how they can continue to work for a company that isn't—and if it would hurt their career.

The hard truth is, most companies are not people-first. They are profit-first or shareholder-first environments. There isn't anything wrong this approach; it's just different.

What makes one company successful will be different from company to company, as will the success path they've chosen. Each company has to decide the tradeoffs they want to make to meet their overall goals and objectives. If you are people-first culture—a true people-first culture—you are likely going to leave some profits on the table. If you are a profit-first culture, you are likely going to miss out on key talent or people opportunities. These aren't bad tradeoffs, just a C-suite decision that has to be made.

Another key point here is that there's a lot of "in between" that companies tend to fall into. It's not an either-or concept at a high level. You can be a people-first company and make money (take Google, for example), just like you can be a profit-first company and have dedicated employees (think about Deloitte: Even though they sell "people-first" solutions, they are a profit-driven company).

We can't influence, especially in a large company, the tradeoff decisions that are made at this level. This is why we're going to focus on the things we can influence—and be confident that being in a profit-first culture, or any culture that isn't "people-first," still provides us with ample opportunity to create wonderful employee experiences.

14

INTERNAL EMPLOYEE EXPERIENCE FRAMEWORK

THE EMPLOYEE EXPERIENCE FRAMEWORK ELEMENTS REMAIN THE SAME whether you're applying them externally or internally: Know, Feel, Act, and Touch. As a reminder, here is how each element is defined:

- **Know** is applied in two different contexts along the journey: What do we need our employees to know at any given time along the journey, and do we know what our employees need to know?
- **Feel** is the stage when we define how we want our employees to feel at that specific point in time—in relation to the company and their overall experience.
- **Act** is when we guide our employees to the next action we want them to take. This is what we want them to actively do: the one next thing.
- **Touch** is the how we actually connect the experience together: the various ways we touch and interact with our employees.

When you are considering the internal employee experience, you can apply the framework at the macro level (company-wide, as shown in Part I) and also at the micro level (which we'll explore in this section). The micro-level application is where most of us can influence change and outcome, and it presents the opportunity to see change and engagement in real time.

This phase of the process is nuanced, as your employees are not just one group of one-size-fits-all, but individuals with varying backgrounds, experiences, tenure, and company-specific interactions. The key when looking at the internal experience is to constantly shift our perspective from leader (or HR, manager, etc.) to employees. We must ensure that we are being the guide—and letting our employees be the hero of the story.

Know that what our employees need will vary based on their tenure and their own personal values and needs at different stages in their lives. We're meeting our employees where they are. We will never be able to engage everyone with our ideal employee experience, as it's still up to each employee to actively engage, but we do want to consider different audiences and how we can reach the majority of our employees with delivering a great employee experience.

When considering the employee experience from an internal employee's perspective, the framework gets even smaller in focus and larger in value, purpose, and impact. We also have more opportunities to reinforce the ideal experience and more opportunities to create negative experiences. While there is more weight behind each experience, because they have engaged with our company and decide to show up each day as a part of our community, employees tend to need more proof of negative experiences to decide to leave. This works in our favor, since we are both getting something out of the equation, but it doesn't mean we can continue to not focus on creating the ideal experience using the framework.

Know

Employees' needs for knowledge once they are employees are constant and ever-changing. And with so many more audiences (each employee can be considered an audience if we want to go very micro), our job of being the guide and crafting the right knowledge points becomes more difficult. Unlike at the macro level, where we can create a company-wide knowledge statement, the framework for employees works best by evaluating each big activity and going from there.

For example, if you work in HR, the activities you want to create micro experiences for are things like annual enrollment, recruiting process, onboarding, performance management (goals), payroll, merit process, talent management, employee engagement survey, and so on. Look at the high-level, high-impact activities, projects, and campaigns (and possibly platforms) that matter most to your employees (and to HR), and start there.

Choose one, then cycle that one through the framework. Once you have your journey mapped out, continue for each consecutive project.

Remember to define both Know statements:

1. What do our employees *need to know* at given time along the journey?
2. What do our *employees need*?

Then evaluate your different audiences if needed. Typically, the best audience to start with is based on tenure. What does someone new to the company need to know, versus someone who has been with your company several years?

Sometimes there are different knowledge needs, such as how the engagement survey process works. If someone has participated in your survey process for several years and you haven't changed anything (you should—but that's another chapter), it's a "rinse and repeat" action for your tenured employees. But a new employee will need to know more context from both knowledge questions: things such as why the company does the survey, what happens to the results, whether it is anonymous, and so on. This is not to say your tenured employees don't need the same information as reminders, but they have more muscle memory around the activity (versus it being a new action).

The most important questions to answer during any internal employee experience audit are: **What's in it for me (the employee) and why do I care?**

Both should be addressed in the Know section—and should be answered in its highest form.

Using the same example, we need to be sure as the guide we're connecting the pieces for the hero regarding the importance of participating in the employee engagement survey. Why? Well, it's important because we make budget decisions based on the responses; we are able to identify culture breakdowns; we get a sense of the pulse of our organization; we can submit our company for Great Places to Work awards, and so on (enter your reason here). But why would an employee care about any of those responses? They don't, so it's the wrong focus point for this section. Instead, through the employee lens, they care about participating because it's one of their only opportunities to have their voice heard; participate in shaping C-suite decisions and culture; and be active members of the company's community. These are the knowledge points that we need employees to know—the value for them, as individual employees, to take time and participate in the survey.

Feel

Using your company's macro-level Feel statement, ensure that you are consistently referring to that high-level feeling and connection with the company. However, just like with knowledge, the emotions we want our employees to feel will vary based on the campaign, project, or situation. There should not be a dramatic swing in the emotions you want to evoke at the macro levels, since you will want to connect the overarching macro emotion to the project-specific one as you go.

Because we want to always connect your employees with the greater company emotional connection/feeling, you will have two feels at the same time. The first will be the company feeling, and the second will be the immediate feeling for the situation. The company-level emotion should be a support feeling—just the connection for us to ensure we're guiding our employees on the right path.

When evaluating the desired emotional connection and feeling for each project, it's critical to put your guide hat on firmly and not let our own biases get in the way. The best way to do this is to start with the macro emotion, then brainstorm how that specific activity will directly connect to the company's macro emotion.

During your brainstorm, the easiest way to do this is to divide a piece paper in half, and complete the activity like this example.

Example: Company's macro emotion is to create a sense of belonging or inclusion.

Goal: Ensure that *everything we do* reinforces the emotion of belonging.

Project: Annual enrollment communications

Micro Emotion for This Project	How it Ties to the Macro Emotion
Knowledgeable	• Provides several communication channels to help employees get the information in their preferred method or learning style • Details are easily available and searchable, not hidden or difficult to find • Can call, email, or chat with a specialist for additional information at any time during annual enrollment
Valued	• Benefits (and available options) meet the needs of employees across all ages, needs, career tenure • Investment by the company shows employee-first thinking and consideration
Protected	• Access to medical (and other) benefits when they need it

Once you have outlined a few options, it's time to view each feeling from the guide perspective. To do this, ask: "How does this emotion [enter feeling brainstorm] connect and bring the employee closer to our company's goals?" Then, you want to put on *your* employee hat and ask, "Does this emotion make *me, as an employee,* feel more connected to the company? Can I relate to how this is bringing me along the journey?"

One of the biggest obstacles you may run into is that your own emotional biases get in the way. The way we see the world from an emotional perspective will absolutely get in the way of us guiding our employees. We will keep ourselves stuck as the hero.

For example, I am not a very emotional or woo-woo person. (I'm working on it.) Things don't tug on my heartstrings, and I don't have a terribly large amount of empathy in general; I come from things from a more practical, logical, or realistic perspective. When I go through the feeling exercise, I have to be sure to not let my own perspective come through. Let's say we were determining the Feel for our performance management process. I may create a list of feelings that include accomplished, knowledgeable, confident, excited, and focused. These are actually a lot more positive than they are in my head, because the list isn't comprehensive. I would want to add things like ready to exit or improve performance and motivated to up-level.

The company wants employees to feel like they accomplished a lot and added value to their bottom line. And they want employees to feel supported if they are underperforming. I would want underperformers to feel motivated to do better or to exit the organization; that's my own practicality getting in the way. In order for me to get to the supported side of the fence, I need to put on my employee hat and consider how I would want to feel if I were deemed an underperformer. I would want to know exactly what went wrong and feel like I have the support I need to improve my performance including resources, leadership, and so on.

If you know that you fall anywhere except in the middle of the emotional spectrum in your own perspective, it's always helpful to have a colleague, friend, spouse, family member—someone else—help gut-check your Feel for each project. Tip: Pick someone who doesn't work in your same role (e.g., outside of HR if you're in it). They will help remove another knowledge bias you have and see things through only an employee lens.

Act

Unlike with the macro experience, the Act step becomes the easiest step in the framework when evaluating things on individual micro levels. Because we are breaking down activities into campaigns, projects, activities, and so forth, there will only be one next action.

You will have one Act for the project as a whole, filled with various needed actions along the way to get your hero to take the final action. Don't try to look at each individual action that the employee needs to take in the middle of the activity for your journey. Those items will be part of how you communicate the campaign/project. Instead, it's one final action.

For example, if you're creating an employee experience map for annual enrollment, the Act is for employees to enroll in benefits. Of course, there are about 20 other things we want employees to do before they take that one final action, but that is the Act for that project. We'll then be responsible for guiding our employees to take the 20 actions in between, through our communication channels.

One quick note here on varying actions based on employee type. If you have one set of actions that leaders need to take versus employees, ideally you would split the project apart and have a framework for each defined audience and activity. One of the best examples of this is performance management (goal-setting and evaluating accomplishment process). What we need leaders to Know, Feel, Act, and Touch is greatly different than what our employees need to Know, Feel, Act, and Touch. Because there is such a gap, this project is best split into two mini-projects: one focused on leaders and one focused on employees.

If you're struggling to determine the one action that needs to be taken, figure out what success looks like for this project. When do you get to check the box that it's complete? What is the point of your company spending time, money, and energy on this activity? These questions should help you define the ultimate Act needed for each project.

Touch

Touch will continue to be the most tangible step in the framework for employees, but it will also expand exponentially, as your internal touchpoints are vast. When you're evaluating an individual micro project, campaign, and so on, you will have multiple internal touchpoints that your employees interact with daily (leaders, email, instant message, phone, intranet, etc.), and, depending on the project, you may have other touchpoints that are specific to the project.

This step is where you may find yourself going down a rabbit hole of outlining the various touchpoints that employees will need to interact with to complete your one action. And worse, it may feel overwhelming when you realize you aren't able to influence many of those touchpoints for change or ideal settings. Don't fret. What you want to do is focus on the *main* touchpoint(s) that your employee will need to touch to accomplish your next action.

Using the annual enrollment example, if our Act is to have employees enroll, the main touchpoint would be our benefits administrator. They absolutely must touch that system (via phone or online) to complete the enrollment action. If you want, you can stop there—although it may provide an incomplete picture of the touchpoints, so your experience may be influenced outside of what you've defined. I would add other touchpoints that support your employee to get to enrollment, such as a total rewards microsite, email/text communications, videos, and webinars. The idea here is to simply inventory the various steppingstones so we can evaluate how we can guide our employees to take our one action.

By doing so, we can indicate the touchpoints we can influence, reinforce the various messages and feelings we want to, and also understand what we may have to work around or within. This helps you focus your energy, time, and money efficiently so you're able to deliver the ideal employee experience and continue to guide your employees.

One final hint: go wide here, not deep. It's more important to know what the touchpoints are than the various times/ways each touchpoint interacts at this stage in the game. We don't want to miss a critical touch, providing more friction or a roadblock, if we can avoid it.

15

YOUR COMPANY CULTURE

AN EMPLOYEE'S PERSPECTIVE

THERE IS NO QUICKER WAY TO ADD FRICTION TO YOUR EMPLOYEE'S experience than misalignment between what you say your culture is and what the *actual* culture is for employees on a daily basis. When we claim our culture—whether it be a statement, a feeling, a buzzword, a practice, or something else—if we are saying, "Our culture is . . .," we are actively placing a stake in the ground and telling everyone who we are and what we believe.

What's ironic about the importance of culture is that no one (with the exception of HR sometimes) knows what culture actually means. In fact, there isn't one standard definition of (work) culture available in the dictionary. It's interpreted differently by each person and company. When we define what culture is for our organization, it has weight. It provides a baseline for your audience to start from and what to expect.

Following that train of thought, when we say something and then the experience and/or reality does not match, our employees think we are lying to them. Or that they aren't "getting it." Or that they must be doing something wrong or working in the wrong area to experience your culture statement.

Let's walk through a few examples of culture statements and rally cries from real companies you would recognize. I've removed their names to protect the guilty parties.

Culture statement 1: Be bold.

This is a great statement and aspiration. It's telling you what to be, it's an action, and it feels motivating when you read it. But other than that, what does being bold actually mean? How can you be bold in your daily work?

Suppose we are able to answer those questions for our own jobs as employees at that company. What then? Are you supported in being bold? Does your manager (and do your senior leaders) encourage bold ideas, innovation, suggestions, approaches, pushback, and more? Are you provided the time and space in your daily job to focus on larger projects and deliverables?

Finally, is being bold rewarded—and, if so, how? Does being bold have a direct connection for each employee to the company's goals and success factors? Is there a reason an employee would care about boldness?

This is just scratching the surface, but you can see how quickly a culture statement can morph into something well outside of what it was designed to be. If you were an employee at the company who wants you to be bold, and then you realize that there is no way for you to do that in your current role, your boss has zero tolerance for new ideas, and the company rewards old systems and processes, how would you feel?

The feeling this company wanted to create is empowerment to spark innovation. Instead, they created frustration when people tried being bold and got shut down, which leads to apathy and, eventually, turnover. All of this because their culture statement is not only ambiguous and unhelpful, but also because it's not rooted in the reality of what employees are able to influence or deliver in their daily roles.

Culture statement 2: Think heads up. (This was commonly referred to internally as "heads-up thinking.")

The phrase *heads up* has me ducking—thinking a ball is being thrown at me.

Employees had no idea what this actually meant and quickly started using it incorrectly, because it didn't resonate. When asked several times, the company further defined the statement roughly: We can't innovate or deliver great work if we're always head-down, focused on doing the work on computers. We need to put our heads up, look and interact around the world, and connect.

This definition irked employees more than the company ever could have expected. They interpreted as follows: So you want me to stop doing the work on my computer that you make me track by the minute, to look up and do what exactly? Oh, and if I do look up, you then reprimand me for not making enough billable hours and not getting the extra work done.

Do you see the contradiction? Do more work, but also be sure to take some time and find white space to connect with colleagues, clients, and the outside world. *How?*

Culture statement 3: We connect passion with purpose.

This statement, or a variation of this sentiment, is quite popular right now. I think it stems from companies wanting to entice Millennials, because so many surveys have indicated that they want to have a purpose and live their passion. That said, this is an example of failed culture statement for several reasons.

First, how does one connect passion to anything—and isn't that different for each person? Let's not even get into how subjective purpose is, too. And how does this apply to a company? And is it helpful for employees, for their own personal passions? This statement says and means absolutely nothing. It's just a few buzzwords put together in hopes that your interest will be piqued.

In addition to the lack of clarity, the biggest mistake this statement makes is that it's a lie for the employees who work there. The statement gives the illusion that employees get to fulfill a sense of purpose with their work and that their passion for ideas, projects, and work will be fostered. But this culture doesn't support any of these things. It's a buttoned-up, hierarchical organization that likes things to be done very systematically, follow orders from the top, and has your typical "corporate culture" mentality. In addition, the company doesn't do anything that would be considered, for most of us, truly purposeful. It's not a nonprofit, it's not saving lives, it's not changing lives; it sells things to companies. Yes, you can argue that their solutions make it easier for *someone* in the organization to do their job (after years of trying to figure out how it all works, just when it's time to upgrade), but there isn't an underlying mission here.

When employees join, they see this company as a possible outlier in their space, having candidates thinking, "Hey, I can work in corporate and follow my passion while feeling fulfilled and purposeful." Yet the everyday working experience is the complete opposite of that. Consider the employee who is seeking those things in their career. What happens next? They leave—quickly, and with a very bad taste in their mouth about the company—and they can't wait to tell everyone how messed up their culture is.

Throughout this chapter, we're going to dive deeper about what culture really is (your employee experience, as we've previously defined it), the gaps between yours and reality, and the various culture components so you can create the experience you want.

Stated Versus Real Culture

Now that you're convinced how a false or unclear culture statement can negatively impact your employee experience and reputation, it's time to do the work to fix this issue. A quick note about your scope or sphere of influence: If you're not able to influence the overall company's culture, you can absolutely create one for the department you work in or lead, your internal client support group, and so forth. Basically, you can create a mini-culture statement within your world instead of relying on big change at the top. It would be better to have your overall company culture reflect accurately across the board, but start where you are.

Start with the Truth

You probably have a sense of how right or wrong your culture statement is, since you are an employee within your organization and feel the rub of it in an ongoing basis. But to understand the work needed, we have to do some detective work.

Find your culture statement. This can be a standalone sentence, a mission, a direction, a compiling of values, or something similar. It's usually found on your company's "About" page or "Careers" page— but also something that you hear from your senior leaders at town halls, in communications, and so on. It's their big initiative and focus —their guiding light to help the company achieve their goals and promises to their constituents.

Once you have the statement, break it down to determine the reality and find the gaps. To do this, ask a series of questions and find common themes. Let's walk through this process using an example.

Culture Statement Example: Delivering mission-critical services and solutions.

<u>**Questions to Ask**</u>

1. Is it clear what this means?

Do you know exactly what the company is trying to say to employees about what the company and employees should care about? Is it ambiguous, directive, aspirational, or something else?

Can employees immediately see or know how they contribute to the culture in their daily work? Can they make that connection, regardless of what motivates them at work?

2. Are they experiencing this statement?

If you surveyed a handful of employees at the company at varying levels, would they agree that delivery is easy, required, focused, and so forth—and that the services and solutions they work on are mission-critical?

We need to consider what the average employee's daily life looks and feels like. Does the statement resonate with them, with their work, their goals, what their manager is asking of them, the direction of the business, the way HR is delivered, and so on?

It's critical for us to be fully honest with how employees at all levels (not just senior leadership) really *feel* about the company and this statement. And it's very important that, for this question, you identify the following: what the experience *actually* is.

3. What is in place supporting this statement?

Most companies don't consider this question when rolling out a culture statement, but it's *how* this culture can be transformed. Evaluating policies, organizational designs, leaders, technology, expectations, employment capacity, decisions, environment, and more will help you identify important gaps and friction points.

I happen to be very familiar with the company culture in our example. Had the senior leadership team asked this question, they would have realized that their culture statement has little to no support from their own internal policies, systems, decisions, and so on. Employees are over capacity after several layoffs, the org structure changes every three to six months (flip-flopping back and forth), line leaders are not able to be true decision-makers, they don't have the systems and tools to deliver things, and more.

This is not to knock their company culture, but to show how *bad* of a culture statement they created. If they asked this question, they would easily find out that their company does not operate in a way that supports delivering mission-critical services and solutions. They *want* to be, but it's not the reality of how they are currently structure.

4. What will get employees to walk across the bridge?

This question is to help you, once you've identified the gaps and friction points, to figure out what needs to happen to make this statement true and resonate. Think of it like the culture statement or senior leadership on one side of the bridge, with your employee standing on the other side. What do they need to Know, Feel, Act, and Touch, to convince them that they belong on the other side, standing next to the senior leaders? What has to be addressed, tweaked, changed, or created to make this statement true?

In our example, this step would include things like an easier technology approval process for systems critical to do their work; repositioning the work that is done to show why it's critical (and to whom); likely changes their staffing practices (hiring, layoff, etc.) to better align client work with people power or, conversely, investments in more automation/systems at a rapid pace.

This step will help you define if the culture statement is the right one and also how to fix it if it's not currently true.

Mission Statements, Core Values, Goals, and More

We've already identified that most companies have a mission statement, core values, goals, and more in place, in addition to or correlation with their culture statement. We can't just say to set those on fire and stop using them because they are wasteful. Instead, we need to understand how to align and leverage them when considering your internal company culture.

First, know this with certainty: The list of things an employee needs to know and resonate with, when it comes to your company's guidelines, is completely unrealistic. We are trying to have our employees behave a certain way that is comprised of many different ideas and sub-ideas and high-level company idealism. As people, we can't be all of those things at once—just like you can't be a people-first culture and profit-first culture at the same time. We have to choose our focus, and then create alignment.

Second, employees will pick and choose what works best for them and how that shows up in their daily work life. What I mean is, they will choose two to three things, at most, that make sense to them or mirror their own values, hopes, dreams, and/or experiences. Know that your list of "culture" things is never going to fully be understood if you continue to have eight different buckets of expectations.

But we can create alignment among the culture statement, the mission, values, and goals—to help our employees focus on the *one* thing that is most important for our company's success.

Using the example above, in addition to their culture statement, here are their core values:

- Client-centricity
- Commitment to excellence
- Trust
- Speed and agility
- Open and inclusive
- Leadership and teamwork

And here's their mission statement: We deliver mission-critical services and solutions on behalf of businesses and governments—creating exceptional outcomes for our clients and the millions of people who count on them.

They are asking *a lot* from their employees to be their ideal employee. They start with the culture statement of delivering mission-critical services and solutions, and then in addition want employees to focus on their clients-first, be excellent, have trust, be fast and inclusive, and work as a team. Um, sure?

Do those core values add value to their culture statement (which is a short version of their mission statement [which makes sense here])? Perhaps an easier way of asking this question is: Do these core values lead to a successful culture statement? Can we draw a direct line between our desired culture and the things we want our employees to show daily?

Maybe? But when you're looking at your company's elements, you want to start with the thing that is most important. The overall Employee Experience Framework is your best starting point, which then leads to your culture statement. Start there, and use this as your guiding light. If we want employees to do/create this culture, how can these other things support that?

If you consider your list of corporate "things" like you would when evaluating a desired action, you know you need to boil it down to just *one next thing*. All of the in-between details and steps are their own touchpoints along the way, but you have to get focused and clear on one idea. The same is true here. Your culture statement becomes the one idea—especially after you've updated it to be true, with the other components being the details in between.

These things can then support *how* you create the culture. How employees exemplify the desired attributes. How policies are created. How decisions are made. Your values become ingrained in the way you do business *because* it leads to your culture statement's success.

Practically, core values can easily be added to performance management, which is goal-setting and performance evaluation; merit processing, which is salary increase based on performance; promotional decisions; employee awards; and so on. The issue becomes when you try to add them to everything, while layering on culture, daily work experience, mission, and more.

Company and Individual Goals

Goals are just a symptom of the larger problem: how you value your employees as contributors to your company's success. It's not clear.

You don't need any additional goal pressure. But wouldn't it be great if your goals actually meant something that you could get excited about each day you show up to work? And as a bonus, leaders and HR can move from the goal police into helping employees feel more connected and grounded to making a true impact—starting now.

Our current goal-setting process—yes, even the cascading of goals —is deeply broken. The issue isn't with how SMART your goals are: It's that your goals don't mean anything. We're often left trying to fit our work and upcoming projects into a broad company culture statement like "Be more innovative" or "Develop consultative acumen."

SMART Goals

SMART goals describe the result that needs to be achieved, not the steps that will be taken, with detailed criteria so you can measure your success.

S: Specific

Goals should be simplistically written and clearly define what you are going to do. This is the what, why, and how of the SMART model. What exactly are you going to deliver? What will the goal accomplish? How and why will it be accomplished?

M: Measurable

Expectations set for goals are clearly written with specific measurements so you can determine success and stay on track.

A: Attainable

Goals should be achievable; they should stretch you slightly so you feel challenged, but be defined well enough so that you can achieve them. You must possess the appropriate knowledge, skills, and abilities needed to achieve the goal. Do you have the necessary knowledge, skills, abilities, and resources to accomplish the goal?

R: Realistic

Goals should measure outcomes, not activities. Relevancy is tied to the business goals and objectives: Why is this goal important to the company and its success? What is the reason, purpose, or benefit of accomplishing the goal?

T: Timebound

Goals should be linked to a time frame that creates a practical sense of urgency or results in tension between the current reality and the vision of the goal. What is the established completion date and does that completion date create a practical sense of urgency?

As an employee yourself, do you actually want to do those things? Of course, you need to figure out what the statement means and how you could possibility deliver that, and then you quickly start considering if that would add any value to the work you have to do in your daily job responsibilities.

Setting goals and having your annual performance rated on these goals is likely not going away (at least not this year) for most of us. Goals need to be set, but the way we approach goal-setting—and HR's commitment to each employee's success—can greatly impact our biggest focus: true employee engagement.

Instead of applying the company's goals or, worse, randomly making your own goals that don't align to your culture statement (ahem, employee experience), you need to set intentional goals within your team and across your company. This type of goal instantly creates a positive employee experience, reinforces our framework goals, and, by default, drives engagement.

To set any goal, where they are at the company, department or individual level, follow these three steps:

Step 1: Inventory and Assess Your Deliverables

Before you can connect meaning to your work and how it impacts the greater good of your company, you need to clearly identify what your job is (and isn't) and the various deliverables and projects you are a part of. Look to last year: What annual events did you lead, what projects did you participate in, what type of employee interaction did you have, and so on?

You need to fully inventory your role to find the nuggets and best examples of how you are contributing. Then look forward: What's expected of you this year, and what has been added to your plate that will enhance your personal growth or your department's success in the coming year?

Likely, you'll end up with well more than the three to five items you're "supposed" to carry as goals. That's okay. We're simply assessing the workload and expectations as of today—which we all know will invariably adjust and shift as the year goes on and competing priorities popup.

Then ask your team members to do this as well.

Step 2: Step Back and Look More Broadly

This is the step that interrupts the typical goal-setting process—and one that will greatly influence our success as an employee and as an HR department. To simplify this step, consider your goals from 30,000 feet above. In other words, consider the broader view of your role and purpose at the company.

What's your reason for doing the work? Why are you in HR (or Marketing, Finance, etc.)? Why do you show up every day? What impact do you want to make this year? How can you best serve your customers?

Big questions, I know—but it's important to consider them if you want to truly change the way you show up each day. This is your "man in the mirror" moment.

It's critical that you consider your true motivation for each question. This isn't for you to share with others but will help you connect your goals and performance that match your motivation and drivers.

Step 3: Create Your Story Snippet

When considering our company's broader goals (or even our department's goals), we're usually left scratching our heads trying to figure out how what we do in our specific department, or what our employees do in their respective departments, actually ties to these concepts. You try to fit your goals into the various buckets or just make up something that doesn't help us get your job done any faster.

In other words, you don't give a hoot about the company's culture initiatives—not because you don't care to improve the culture, but because your company isn't giving you a reason or a way to find meaning and correlation between the work you do and the success of the company. That's where your Story Snippet comes in.

What is your Story Snippet?

It's a simplified version of what is traditionally known as your **brand as an employee.** It connects you with, and gets you excited about, the company you work for. And then it gets you excited to be working in your department, for your manager, on your team, and so on. It's why you want to show up each and every day for work—other than the most obvious (you need to get paid!).

Your Story Snippet contains four parts:

1. Who: your deliverables, or team, or clients
2. What: the problem you are solving
3. Why: what they care about
4. Result: how their lives improve

From here, you'll have your role and deliverables clearly defined, your company goals are noted, you understand your own motivation, and you have your personal brand (simplified). Alone, these are just steps leading you to a better starting point for your goals.

By understanding your Story Snippet, you will have a clear direction on the right goals to start with and why they are important to *you*. Yes, your goals should be SMART, but part of your goal needs to always tie back to why it's important to you—and why it's important for your company.

Here's an example of a short Story Snippet for an HR manager using the four pasts as outlined previously:

1. Clients: Senior leaders of Marketing and IT; and individual employees within these organizations.
2. Providing strategic HR support, guidance, and consulting to improve the connection between employees and HR.
3. Want people-related information that is accurate and easy to find, when they need it (urgency) and a trusted advisor and partner who is an expert in the HR function.
4. We become part of the business, not a standalone department. Employees will get the information they need, when they need it; HR's reputation improves. Leaders will have the support they need, feel confident in their HR activities, increase positive employee experiences and engagement.

Go to bettHR.com/story to download the Story Snippet template.

LET'S FIX IT: HR!

Unlike all of the books out there on how to increase employee engagement (the theories, the ideas, 1,001 ways, surveys, and so on) improving the employee experience is a concrete, step-by-step process, with almost-instantaneous and long-lasting results. To help you do that for your organization, we tackle the most common employee campaigns, projects, and touchpoints, so you can start implementing these changes right now.

A quick note: Improving your employee experience is not going to fix all of what's wrong in your company or in your HR department. It's not going to eliminate bad managers (although it will help you identify where they are and next steps). It's not going to fix your senior leader disconnect (although it will help them see where it is and how you can align it). In other words, it's not a magic bullet that will change the DNA of your organization overnight. But it will move the needle on the number of engaged employees in your organization, change the external and internal reputation of your company, help HR and leaders manage more effectively, and spend your budget dollars more efficiently.

The guidance, action plans, and best practices in this section are based on what's been successful for our clients (and us!) over the past several years. We have tested them with companies from mom-and-pop shops to Fortune 500 companies, from coast-to-coast in the U.S. (and even a few companies in Canada). This works; all you need to do is apply it.

Let's fix it, then, shall we?

Onboarding Process

The onboarding process is the first internal experience your new employees have with your company—and it is the first true employee experience they have. We've previously reviewed all of the steps leading to this point, which absolutely help shape your employee's first impressions, but this is your standout moment.

Surprisingly, this step seems to be broken at most companies (even companies that have followed a suggested process or sent welcome gifts). A piece of the onboarding process tends to work well, and yet, as a process, there are few companies who do it well.

Regardless what your current onboarding process is, it can be improved to better fit your ideal employee experience (culture)—and add even more value, connection, and relationship-building for your new team members.

At a high level, every onboarding process needs to address the following four items:

1. Do I feel welcomed and part of the team?
2. Do I have the tools I need to do my job?
3. Is it clear what I'm responsible to do and accomplish?
4. Is there a plan to get me to success?

You'll see Know, Act, and Touch clearly identified, and Feel varying based on your company's approach (although it tends to land on the excited spectrum).

In absence of these four items, employees will start to build negative thoughts and experiences about your company when they are just getting started. This is the quickest way to disengagement from day one, and none of us want that.

Most companies approach onboarding in a segmented fashion because, frankly, it's easier and we've grown into the onboarding process through a series of band-aid solutions. We all know this isn't working—and it absolutely will not work as our workforce and work environment continue to change.

Step 1: Create an Onboarding Owner

Instead of having onboarding handled by various people and departments, designate an owner.

The current state tends to look something like this: Talent Acquisition (TA; Recruiting) manages the offer letter and the background work needed for the candidate to turn into an employee, and then they hand off the process to the hiring manger to handle day one and beyond. And there is almost *always* a gap of information, process, requirements, knowledge, and so on for your future employee.

In some cases, you may provide the hiring manager a checklist of things they need to do (request IT access, create an onboarding plan, set goals, etc.), but it's still up to the manager to understand the steps and take action. And we all know that individuals respond in their own unique way, creating an inconsistent experience.

Based on best practice, the best owner for this process tends to reside in Talent Management or an Integrator. Why? Because they have the most skin in the game: Their jobs depend on creating engaged employees.

Here's the good news: This isn't a full-time job for most companies; the scope will depend on your company size and how many people you tend to onboard annually. The role will take some time up-front (we've seen about three to six months to set up with focus), and then it runs in the background for the most part.

This is true because you systemize the onboarding process, creating a standard operating procedure and various online processes/systems to make it easy to do. And no, you don't need to add a significant spend to make this happen.

Step 2: Dig into the Current Process

The new owner of the process will need to gather information about the current process to understand what exists, what's currently happening, where the gaps and friction points are, and the ideal way to move forward. To do this, you talk to the current partners of the onboarding process (Talent Acquisition, a few hiring managers, IT) and, most importantly, new employees (more on this shortly).

Once the feedback is gathered, the process of rebuilding begins— starting with crafting the employee experience journey for onboarding and clearly identifying the Know, Feel, Act, and Touch for this project.

From there, the process owner should outline the new process and identify various steps of knowledge along the way. Then, systemize.

Step 3: Systemize

Using your company's preferred online resource for projects (maybe it's your learning system, a project management system [like Asana], the intranet, a survey tool, etc.), you create repeatable steps that your TA and hiring managers must complete during the onboarding process.

By having an online process, with an overseer/approver, you will by default create more buy-in and obligation to completion. This is a total win—once you get past the change management growing pains.

At a minimum, your onboarding process/system should include the following:

- Day one expectations
- Team introductions
- Goal-setting

- Resources kit
- Onboarding surveys

Day One Expectations

This is what an employee and their hiring manager should expect on day one. This includes things like where to go, when to arrive, what to do when you get there, how much time should be devoted to certain activities, other people who should be a part of day one, learning activities, HR activities, paperwork, welcoming activities or expectations, and a plan for the next week.

If you create the answers to these as a standard template and level of expectations, including where the hiring manager and your new employee (different versions if needed) are able to access them, day one becomes a lot less scary and keeps your new employee in the feeling you want to reinforce.

Team Introductions

This part is focused on welcoming and including the new employee. Determine the ideal way to do that for your company, and then create it as a standard expectation and template. Things to consider include a new employee email to the team (or company), team meeting and one-on-one meetings, gift or promo items for the new employee, a team roster, and organizational charts.

Goal-Setting

Clearly define when the new employee's goals need to be set, how they will be set (approach, cascading, etc.), the system to input them, details around what goals mean, and how they will be monitored. This is critical, even if you want to roll your eyes at your company's goal-setting/performance management process, because employees—particularly new employees—need to feel confident about what's expected of them. Ambiguity may be great for some employees, but only after they trust the leader, system, and company, to be able to explore it. Knowing exactly what success looks like and how it is measured goes a very long way in this process.

Resources Kit

Put your resources in one, easy-to-access place for your new employees. Everything. It may only be a resource used by new hires, but it is worth it. Add it to an intranet page (if your employees all have easy access to it day one), create a PDF, or put it on an external website that is password-protected. Basically, share where to go for what—in all cases. Have a payroll question? Go to this website or call this number. Not sure what to do in general, can't access something, have a question? Whatever it is, create a kit for your new employee that is provided day one.

Onboarding Surveys

Touching base with your new employees and their hiring manager is critically important. No one is better suited to tell you exactly what is going right or wrong in your onboarding process than someone who not only just went through it and who also comes with an outsider's perspective. If you are not asking for their input, you are missing out on critical information that can easily improve your experience.

Best practice is to reach out for feedback in 30 and 90 days, and the questions you ask are critically important and always confidential/anonymous. Before I walk through suggested questions, let's walk through a few examples of *bad* questions that companies tend to include (and why they won't work). Awareness of these will help you craft the best questions for your organization.

What Not to Ask

- Are you satisfied/happy with your new role?
- This question will not get you any useable feedback because you are asking a new employee, who is depending on their job to pay their bills, if they like their new job. There is really no incentive for your new employee to answer this honestly in fear of their role.
- How did the onboarding process go?
- Not only is this extremely broad, but it also isn't fair. If they had a bad experience at one step, but a good experience overall, how does one answer that—and what feedback are you actually learning to improve the process?
- Is the job what you expected it to be?
- Great information for us to know, but if the answer is *no,* most people will be uncomfortable with saying so.

Suggested Questions for Optimal Feedback

Instead, here are some questions to ask and a few general rules. First, ask open-ended questions versus leading or yes/no questions. If you need more survey-style questions versus text-questions, use Likert scales (varying degrees of connection [extremely agree, agree, neutral, disagree, strongly disagree], for example, or a scale from 1 to 10). The best feedback that you can act upon, however, will always be open-ended text responses. You can create your survey with all open-ended text questions, or you can use scales and provide a text question at the end of each section—particularly if they didn't respond positively.

- Can you share ways in which you felt welcome when joining the organization (and the negative of this question)?
- What would have been helpful to you during the onboarding process that was not available?
- What information do you wish you knew when you joined the company?

- What went well (and what could be improved as a separate question)?
- How can we improve the onboarding experience (or your first 30 days)?
- What suggestions do you have for us to make the new employee transition easier?
- Was there something during your onboarding process (or first 30 days) that could have worked better?

If you want some "quick" yes/no questions, these types of questions tend to work best:

- Did you have the information you needed on day one?
- Did you feel supported throughout the onboarding process?
- Do you feel supported by your manager (and/or new team) in your new role?
- Are the expectations for your role clearly defined?

Once you have this information, you can easily identify what's working and what's not—and quickly update your systems/processes to adjust accordingly.

HR Systems and Payroll

The next process that all employees interact with is your HRIS. Your HRIS is the technology platform your company uses for things including personnel files, employment records, compensation, and payroll. You may have different systems for each one of these things— which isn't ideal but is likely something you're unable to influence in the immediate future. Instead, we'll work with these systems your company already has in place and be sure to consider how these systems may meet the needs of HR or IT and also be a huge friction point for our employees.

Quick note: If you're not in HR, you still have a lot to contribute in this section. You're an employee, and as an employee, you interact with these systems often and can partner with your HR team or senior leader to help implement these solutions.

The most important thing for our employees when interacting with your HRIS and/or payroll system is: Is my information correct in the right places so I can get paid easily? At the end of the day, compensation is the thing that employees care most about.

And once that is set up, employees move into ongoing maintenance or updating their details. Can they do that easily and without issue—and if not, is there someone to contact to help?

When evaluating your HRIS, forget about the bells and whistles that your big consulting partners are trying to sell you and make sure you have the basics working well before doing *more*. If you've been in HR (or an employee!) for any amount of time, you've likely seen your fair share of HRIS interfaces (Brassring, Oracle, PeopleSoft, Workday, UtlimateSoftware, ADP, Successfactors—the list is endless) because what we need our HRIS to do continues to change and evolve as our workforce does. Your HR team, as a trend, invests in a system upgrade every three to five years, to incorporate all of the shiny new objects.

And with each update or change in software or release, employees have to relearn the system—starting with the basic question again: Will I get paid? Having great HRIS systems in place is a *wonderful* thing. Being behind in software is painful, but we need to achieve the following goals before updating and while maintaining.

Using the Employee Experience Framework, here's what your HRIS needs to accomplish:

- Know: one secure location to provide their details and that will result in them getting paid
- Feel: confident that their information is secure, accessible, and updateable if needed
- Act: submit your information to our system of record
- Touch: ideally, one system that can feed into your other

systems if needed, but a clear entry point to input and find
their employment information and details (HRIS system)

When you're evaluating your current HRIS as part of this process,
or if you're about to update or purchase new software, here are best
practices to reinforce your ideal employee experience.

First, make sure it's easily accessible. If it's behind a log-in, make
sure it's easy for employees to know and reset if needed (it's not often
that employees log on to update their address). If it's a single-sign-on
link, does that function only within the firewall, and do all employees
have quick access to it? Make sure it's accessible. This is critically
important and where you should actually invest your spend to make it
very easy for your employees.

Obviously, this type of information needs to be behind a log-in, but
make sure that you're placing it behind the right one (or it will create a
lot of questions and call center calls or help desk emails). When an
employee wants or needs access to this data, it feels urgent and will
ramp up their frustration if they aren't able to figure it out.

Another consideration is how many clicks your employees will
need to go through to get to their information. With any type of online
user interface, the fewer number of clicks, the better the experience.

I can think of several HRIS systems that I've used as an employee
with varying degrees of clicks and ease of process. For example, with
Oracle, it looked very clunky and it was unclear where I needed to
click once I was logged in. This was likely due to the design or
customizations the company chose, but I had to click from the landing
page (what appears when you sign on), to "Home," to "My Personal
Information," to "Compensation or Data." Interestingly, I learned that
this information was actually fed from a different HRIS (Ultimate), so
you had to make changes in Ultimate but would look at the information
in Oracle. Super-confusing.

Workday has improved a lot with their interface, and their clicks
have become more streamlined, especially if you invest in their off-the-
shelf solution. Same with Ultimate. The point here is to evaluate each

solution, product, software, or system, through this lens: How quickly will an employee get there?

Second, the language you are using on your HRIS is way too confusing (aka "HR speak"). As HR professionals or as leaders in the organization, HR terms are second nature and carry meaning with them. But they don't have any value and don't translate to your employees, because—surprise—they aren't HR experts! Scrub your HRIS for any and all HR speak and language. For example, take the word *compensation.* Instead, use *pay, salary,* or *what you earn.* The only time you should consider using the word *compensation* is when you're showing a total compensation statement or chart, which encompasses all of their pay details, bonuses, healthcare, and so forth. And even then, you can insert pay or *pay value* for the word *compensation.*

And if your HRIS has a leader interface for leaders to track information and details about their employees, be sure to use language there that makes sense to non-HR people. Words like *turnover, terminations,* and *cycle process* leave a lot of room for interpretation and there are easier, more relatable words to use (e.g., *employees leaving the organization; progress status*).

Third, your HRIS should provide you in HR (or leaders) the ability to create meaningful metrics for your organization. (We'll tackle the employee side of this, in the upcoming Total Rewards section.) Your HRIS should be the number-one resource for HR and leaders of information and data that will directly influence your ability to drive the company's profit margin. If your HRIS does not make this information readily available or easy to access, you are missing out on critical information.

Note: Not all HRIS reporting information and data are created equal, and simply using their dashboard will not help you evaluate the specific HR needs. To be successful doing this and creating meaningful metrics without being a data analyst, you need to take the data and following the Storytelling for HR™ process.

Go to bettHR.com/storytelling to learn more about Storytelling for HR.

Total Rewards

"Total rewards" is defined as the comprehensive list of compensation, benefits, perks, offerings, and programs you provide to your employees. This term started with the rise of employee engagement as total rewards was seen as a way to attract, retain and engage top talent.

Its popularity, and perhaps unique components, grew even more when Google came onto the scene. They are the first company most people think of when thinking about broad total rewards programs. Google's senior leaders/founders knew that they needed top talent to grow and that their employees would be working long, hard hours. To help offset that cost, Google invested in providing other perks to not only make it feel like a win to employees, but also to keep employees on campus as long as possible. (Perhaps evil genius at work?)

Today, total rewards, and what it encompasses, has become a big part of being an employee and for HR, attracting, retaining, and engaging talent. And it is usually your company's biggest investment —not just HR's biggest spend (which it is).

With this level of investment comes a lot of responsibility. Few companies approach their total rewards spend correctly or effectively. Not every company can or should be like Google; that doesn't make sense. It works for Google because they are very focused on investing correctly in their employee experience to retain their specific set of talent. For you, it's learning how to apply the best practices to your own company, which will lead to success.

First, what is your company's total rewards strategy? To find this out or put one together, consider what your pay practices are. Are you competitive in the marketplace? Where do you stack up in the pay range/scale reports? Are you known for paying well (or not)? Remember: There aren't any right or wrong answers here; we're just gathering information. In addition to your pay practices, explore what your company provides for benefits (medical, dental, vision, supplemental, financial, wellness, etc.). How robust are your offerings, and how expansive are they?

Second, what's your differentiator? What is the benefit (or benefits) that your company over-indexes on that is enticing to candidates and employees, as a real win? Here are some examples:

- AT&T provides a very strong medical program with *very* low employee premiums. They were at $0 contributions until just a few years ago. Now for an outstanding medical plan, their monthly premiums can be less than $100 for individual coverage. It's a standout, especially within their industry.
- American Express has a very generous parental leave policy that they implemented well before the market. In 2017, they rolled out a 20-week paid leave program. In addition, they focus in on this area by also providing reimbursement (up to $35K!) for adoption, surrogacy, fertility treatments, and more. Their differentiator is how they support their new parents.
- The Clorox Company has a market-leading 401(k) plan that matches contributions up to 4% of pay (which vests immediately) and an annual contribution of 6% of pay (which vests over five years). That's well outside of the market, which currently is trending at a 2.7%[9] match—with many companies decreasing their match dollars as a whole.

These are just a few examples. What does your company invest in as their differentiator? Be sure to consider salary, bonuses, paid time off, remote work policies, sabbaticals, and more. Remember that your company is paying for these things, so you want them to be used and properly selected.

Now, let's break it down through the Employee Experience Framework, knowing that money in their pocket is *always* going to be the most important factor for total rewards. This means not only how much you pay, but also how much money employees can save through your offerings.

- Know: what your differentiator is and how much money is going into my pocket and being saved
- Feel: on the spectrum from comfortably compensated (total compensation) to eased of money worries
- Act: constant reinforcement of the total rewards and how they are adding value (Know section) every day to your employees
- Touch: clearly defined touchpoints and systems, if a standalone is not reasonable (Ideally, you have one place where employees can see, at their fingertips, their total rewards in value and opportunity.)

Outside of base pay, total rewards is a significant component of the overall employee experience. We know that most people work to earn income—which total rewards is partially comprised of. But in addition to base pay, money saved, additional perks, great benefits, and so forth can be significantly important to your employees.

When you're looking for a job, what are you thinking about, asking about, hoping for—outside of base salary? I want to know about time off, retirement planning (matching in particular), and remote working/flexibility. Many candidates I interview want to know what the medical plans are, the types of plans available, and premium costs. I've had friends and family members care deeply about things across the board: pension, bonus potential, deferred compensation, fertility benefits, and more. The point is, people have different needs depending on where they are in life. While your company cannot provide the absolute best rewards for every single individual, you can have a differentiator (or a few of them) to compete in the marketplace.

The best way to find out which ones to *continue to invest in* or over-invest in, is *not* for HR/Benefits/Finance to decide. That will lead to failure faster than not investing in the right total rewards. Instead, you want to refer back to your macro Employee Engagement Framework first, then ask your employees.

Caution: You know how much your total rewards means to you? It means that much to each employee, so asking them about your total rewards programs is very sensitive. Employees' knee-jerk reaction, if the question is not positioned properly, is to think you are looking for ways to take away various benefits or perks—which may be the outcome based on their input, but this is a fact-finding mission only. While you don't need to spend six-figures to get a consult in and do a "this or that" survey, this is one area in which you will benefit from having some outside guidance on, to be sure to stay away from potential road bumps.

Go to bettHR.com/survey to learn more about how to set-up a total rewards survey.

Performance Management

Performance management is an umbrella term that encapsulates your performance review process, goal-setting and measuring, talent management reviews, and more. Basically, it's how your employees are performing and meeting the stated expectations. For some companies, there is also a pay component, called merit, that is tied to performance. Merit itself would be covered under total rewards but is determined by an employee's performance.

While most companies still follow a loose standard of performance management, companies have been exploring different ways to measure performance outside of the annual review process and associated ratings with outdated bell curves. If you work at a company that is doing something outside of the traditional performance management process and it's successful, you are a *very* rare breed. Because it's still the most common approach, that's what we will break down today.

Before we start, let's review some perspective and insight into the performance management process to get us all on the same page. First, it's broken and inefficient. Even if your company has all of the right elements in place, performance management is still hard to do well across the board because it relies on so many different elements and participants. Second, once a year is not nearly frequent enough to be effective. Third, everyone—leaders, managers, and HR—dreads performance reviews. They are way too time-consuming if done well, so therefore most aren't completed properly. And finally, the approach of ranking your employee's performance across a bell curve distribution, in order to solve your merit budgeting issues, sucks. For everyone. But it does appease the budget issues, so most have to work within a version of this framework (because numbers are real).

All of those things aside (I know: That's a lot of big blocks to ignore), let's start with why the performance management process is important for the employee experience. When we reviewed onboarding, we outlined how important it is for new employees to know what is expected of them, how success will be measured, and what those conversations will look like. The same is true for your employees on an ongoing basis. We know that employees want to feel connected and find meaning in the work that they do—and a big piece of that is how they are adding value to the company. The easiest way for employees to connect with this is through their goals—and clearly identifying how the work they do every day contributes to the success of their goals and the company's achievements.

It may feel a bit archaic in approach, but it gives us something to visually see and refer to when we have a bad employee experience or interaction, or just a bad day. It reaffirms our personal why statement (to learn more about how to find your why, I recommend reading *Start with Why* by Simon Sinek). It also eliminates a very important variable that can take up a lot of space in your employee's brains: Am I on track? And am I doing it right? In the absence of this knowledge and comfort, our brains create their own stories, and we lose a lot of time and productivity worrying about that, instead of focused on delivering and innovating.

You've probably experienced this variable in your career. I have, particularly when I had a boss who wasn't comfortable giving feedback. She was very polite and never directly said what was and what wasn't working, so I was constantly questioning if what I was doing was right and helpful. It caused so much angst and ill-will toward her (whom I happened to like very much as a person), and it led to so many negative experiences in my own journey that I ended up leaving the company. Even though her boss provided direct feedback to me, most of which was positive and reaffirming, it wasn't from the person ultimately responsible for my success at the company. I left in part because it wasn't clear, from her, if my performance was adding value.

The most important thing to remember for this process, as it relates to the employee experience and creating positive experiences, is that employees want to feel connected and like they are adding value to the company.

Let's break it down through the Employee Experience Framework.

- Know: exactly how what I am doing and working toward will help the company thrive; how that is going to measured; and how information will be shared
- Feel: confident in my capabilities and next steps to success and part of a community
- Act: strive for achieving my goals—to ultimately support the company's success
- Touch: clearly defined touchpoints, systems, processes, and ongoing conversation templates/requirements

The requirements for performance management at your company will vary, but here are some best practices to consider.

Goal-setting needs to be tied to the experience; we outlined how to do this in Chapter 15. In addition to having meaningful goals, feedback needs to be ongoing and more structured, helping managers who are uncomfortable with feedback to still provide it.

To complete full-blown performance reviews more than once a year is a difficult ask for many companies. Instead, what we've seen work very well is to capture feedback in an ongoing basis—either "always on" or quarterly, through surveys. Make it easy to complete, capture relevant feedback related to the company's experience and the employee's capabilities, and include the option for text responses. Send the anonymous survey to partners, coworkers, managers, clients, and so forth—internally or externally. The data will allow you to capture more real-time feedback and provide information to be delivered in an ongoing basis.

Another approach is one-on-one meetings—and feedback templates for these meetings. I strongly believe that meeting with your manager one-on-one, at least every two weeks, is critically important to improve the employee experience. It builds the relationship and provides the space for feedback. But you need to provide a template or expectations to be covered during these meetings, or leaders will continue as they are now. The easiest way to include feedback is by providing S/TARs.

S/TAR stands for: Situation or Task; Action; Result

If you've heard of S/TARs, it's likely from learning about behavioral interview techniques, but it is easy to apply to delivering feedback as well. If you are giving feedback, or asking for feedback, you'll want it broken down in a S/TAR to make easier to see what's going on.

Here's a typical feedback example: The project seems to be going well. Keep up the good work.

Here's S/TAR feedback: The time-tracking project (S/T) met this week's deadline when you shared the report (A). I'm pleased to know this is on-track and our client partners will be receiving the graphs on time (R).

Which one is clearer and would help you understand what to keep doing?

Typical feedback example #2: I received some feedback from a team member that you were out of line during a recent call.

S/TAR version: During a recent call on project snowflake (S/T), a team member reached out to share with me some concerns with your tone during the meeting. Specifically, when you were telling the client that we weren't able to complete the task and you've reviewed it with them several times already in a perceived snippy tone (A). While I understand your point of view, it's important that our client feels heard and supported at every touchpoint and that we're doing our very best to maintain an even keel at all times (R).

Which one is clearer and would help you know exactly where the breakdown was?

This isn't a skill that most of us are comfortable with, because we don't tend to practice this muscle. Instead, we ignore the situation, bury it until annual review time, don't think it's worth the effort, or don't want to be confrontational (or break a team member's confidence). By doing things the same way we currently are, we're not adding any value to our employees—or their experience.

In example #2, will the employee feel a negative experience? Yes. But it's clear what needs to be addressed and they can work on it. If it were me (and I have been on the end of that conversation before), I'd be wondering, "What meeting? What did I say? Is someone out to get me?" and so on. Being clear and truthful will help reinforce the emotions we want employees experience as a whole, even if they're having a bad moment.

Go to bettHR.com/star to download the S/TAR template.

Learning and Development (Training)

Having a robust and helpful learning and development program (L&D) or a series of training programs tends to be an area that is an either/or for companies, but can deliver so much added value to your employee experience for the effort. L&D as a thoughtful activity can provide your employees with several positive touchpoints and connections, especially if they are able to advance a skill, knowledge area, or their career. Instead, most companies aren't intentional about this area or only provide legally required training.

When it comes to L&D, you have a few options, including the following most popular paths:

Have an in-house L&D group/person to ensure legally required and HR-specific trainings (new hire, etc.) are in place. If the team is robust with a lot of experience and a budget, this group can also provide training within different teams or departments, focused on company-related information or broader career skills. The upside here is that your trainers are part of the culture and experience, with insider's knowledge. The downsides are that when budgets are tight, this is one of the first things cut, and their knowledge well is only as deep as their own personal skill set.

Purchase/subscribe to an off-the-shelf L&D program and trainings. Over the past few years, this option has become increasingly popular, as it can be expensive to create your own training programs when there are so many companies and platforms delivering the same training online. This is ideal for things like your legally mandated training programs—with a caveat: Most of these trainings are *terrible* and you will lose the attention (and respect!) of your employees, if you require them to sit through them year after year. Be sure to get feedback on the programs you are considering to see if they fall into the lame or helpful category. Also, you may be missing out on addressing company-specific lingo, issues, processes, and so on. Depending on the site your purchase from, you have a potential risk (small for the larger names in this space) to have poor talent teaching your employees. This type of training isn't ideal as your L&D strategy or the only training available for your employees.

Define training for different roles/departments that are delivered through various sources. About 10 years ago, before online learning was popular and easy to access, this is the way most companies delivered training if they invested in L&D. There are still many companies that have cherry-picked the best training and delivery channels for different things and provide employees with options based on how they want to grow their career.

When creating the ideal experience for L&D, start with your budget and what talent you have within your organization. Having more money would be great, but that's not always feasible, so start with what you can influence, just like you do with every other step of this process.

Then, outline what the Employee Experience Framework will be for your L&D program. Most will look something like this:

- Know: why this training is important to the company, and how I can leverage it to grow my career and knowledge
- Feel: eager and excited to grow and have time to invest in myself
- Act: complete the next best training—from your defined training plan
- Touch: one place to go to seek available training, even if delivered in various channels (a catalogue of sorts)

Once you have this defined, create different L&D opportunities to deliver on your above promise. That starts with a training plan. Most companies, if they have an online learning system, are able to easily assign all employees certain training based on their role, title, or grade level. But it's a lot easier to do it once per year and have it run on autopilot, versus having to consider it with each employee or, worse, have it fall off the list.

As a department, create a learning plan based on role and/or level, and apply it across the board. For example, all employees will need to complete these trainings annually (in the U.S.): sexual harassment, ethics, code of business conduct. Any company-specific trainings (new-hire orientation, performance management overview, your ombudsman office procedures, etc.) would be part of your list.

Then, pre-define by role and/or level. Leaders at all levels should be enrolled in helpful leadership courses (note: More than one here is intentional). HR employees may need to be enrolled in company HR-specific practices to learn your philosophy or employee experience framework for your HR departments. R&D employees may need to be enrolled in research standards, document retention, and compliance training.

These are examples, but consider what skills and knowledge sets your employees will need to be effective in their role at your organization, particularly as they grow with you. Have that pre-defined so employees are choosing from a path (versus all of your menu offerings). This is especially important if you have an online learning service that allows your employees to enroll in anything. That's not a bad thing, but you want to be sure employees are minimally getting the training they need—not just what they want.

Now that you've spent time and an investment (or re-investment) in L&D, the key factor here is changing the conversation internally around training opportunities. I have worked at several companies that have invested in learning programs, but it is near impossible for you to get your manager to approve your absence to attend the training. Or worse, employees are expected to do it on their own time or use a vacation day.

Conversely, I've worked at and with companies that not only invested deeply in L&D, but also committed time and accountability around it. To no one's surprise, companies that approach learning from this perspective have a much higher percentage of key talent as employees than do companies that put forth minimal effort.

This fact alone is a good conversation point for helping your senior leaders become more intentional around the investment in L&D: money and time. Factors like your employee engagement survey, employee feedback, and the performance management process will also point out the level of need or missing points here.

L&D may feel like a sunken cost, but when it comes to your employee experience, it is one of the easiest ways to create and establish ongoing positive employee touchpoints that are all about the employee (in their perspective). It also elevates your company's talent, knowledge base, expectations, collaboration, and critical thinking. Because learning is all about the employee as an individual, there is a very easy story to get them over the bridge: It's something the company is investing in, for them, specifically.

Employee Engagement Surveys

Employee engagement surveys, tactics, or pulse checks are commonplace at most companies, particularly those with more than 1,000 employees. When engagement surveys first came on the scene about 25 years ago, they were a lot less advanced than they are today, but the same premise is still in place. Use a survey to find out what employees are thinking to gauge their level of engagement with the company. We've already outlined why this approach doesn't work, but as it's the only way most companies are asking for feedback consistently from employees, we want to be sure to leverage it in the best way possible.

These surveys will provide you with information and data, regardless of their engagement influence or outcomes. It's understanding how to use this survey to your advantage, to help create positive employee experiences, that is critical to their success.

Most of us aren't able to influence, especially in a short amount of time, the survey vendor or questions asked, so we will assume the following restraints:

- You are using questions that are broad and based on your vendor's survey pool,
- The questions are the same or similar year after year (at least for the past few years), and
- The survey is administered online and is anonymous.

If your variables are different, that's okay. Use your variables for your baseline. These are the ones that we run across most commonly.

The most important thing for you to know about employee engagement surveys is that employees only care about this: Why would I bother to provide feedback? Will I be retaliated against for being honest? Will leaders make any changes based on my feedback? Basically, why is this worth my time?

Our current perspective and approach to these surveys have us in HR being the hero. We want to learn information first, because it's something we are required by our boss to do annually, but also to see at a high level where things are. And once we get the results, we quickly remove ourselves from the equation and let managers manage the results and create "action plans" to increase engagement.

Think that process through for just a moment. We are asking non-experts to analyze the results and then try to fix the very things that they made break—and didn't care enough to fix on their own. It's never going to work. In addition, you usually have senior leaders in one of two camps: I want to read everything—all verbatim—and fully understand what's going on, and I don't have time; remove the open-ended questions.

I have both worked for and with CEOs in both camps. Neither is easy to work with on this topic. Leaders who want to know everything tend to synthesize results with their own biases and don't get the critical details right, want to over- or under-explain things, and/or never respond because it's too much. In the second camp, you slight your employees because they *want* to tell you what's on their mind in their own words and then are told, "No thanks. What you have to say isn't important."

See how that fails for all?

Starting from that perspective, you want to find the right balance to get your employees' feedback through the Likert scale questions and open-ended text, but also create a way to summarize and share the important information (more on that in a moment).

Just like we do any other project, start with the Employee Experience Framework. For employee engagement surveys, it will tend to look something like this:

- Know: why should I bother taking my time to do this and will anything be done with the results?
- Feel: open to sharing their feedback and safe that it will be received anonymously/constructively
- Act: complete the survey intentionally
- Touch: online link that can anonymize participants

Once you have that in place for your project, take inventory of what is in place and what can and can't be changed in this process. Are the questions grouped by topic or core value? What are the questions?

Then, draw a line between what is there, and what is important to the company and your employee experience. You will find some gaps for sure, but it's what we have to work with that's important.

Earlier I shared why having your leaders "own" engagement is a bad idea. Now that we're going to review best practices for how to tackle your employee engagement surveys, remember that we need to shift the way you view employee engagement action plans and activities.

I know, I know: We want our leaders to own the process—to be accountable. People are engaged and stay at their company because they love their boss . . . right? Sure, your leaders need to play an active role in leading and engaging their employees. But HR needs to be strategic in their guidance—and help get true results. Because yes, a bad boss sucks and makes you want to peace out—but so does a bad company, which is the result of the piling up of negative employee experiences. Let's not forget that.

Knowing that, here's how to create an effective employee engagement action plan.

Step 1: Create Your Essentialism Goal

Unless you have read the book *Essentialism* by Greg McKeown, you likely have no idea what I'm talking about here. (You should read this book. It's great for finding your focus and determining what's important.)

The Cliff's Notes version for this first step is this: determine what are the singular focus and desired outcome for increasing your employee engagement. This is your experience *why*.

Why is it critical for engagement to be increased? What are you trying to solve? Or avoid? Or fix? What is the one outcome that is necessary for engagement to be deemed high?

It sounds easy. That just means you aren't digging to the actual Essentialism goal them. Dig deeper and ask, "So what?"

If you skip this step, you won't be able to deliver results that have any sort of meaning/value. In other words, you'll be in the same place you are right now and lacking strategic delivery here. This helps set the stage as to why this is an important HR activity versus something you are doing year after year because you have the budget for it.

For example, here is the Essentialism goal one of my clients set:

Driving employee engagement will help us become an
employer of choice in their industry and significantly decrease
key talent turnover by at least 10%.

This means that everything they do from this step on is laser-focused on how to decrease key talent turnover and become an employer of choice in their industry. If the actions, activities, and results don't align with that goal, then they leave them on the table and move on.

Your Essentialism goal will narrow your focus to ensure results. It will feel strange because you are no longer thinking about getting everything more than 90% or targeting all of your lowest scores, regardless.

If it doesn't match your goal, it's superfluous.

Step 2: Find Your Outliers

With your Essentialism goal in mind (always), review your results through the lens of identifying outliers. Which things are you currently doing really well to support your goal? Conversely, what areas are you not meeting expectations to support your goal?

Identify things that are outside of the average result—by category and by question. Your standard deviation will vary based on your results, but you want to view the numbers with a questioning perspective. Is that interesting? Why is that different? That's not quite aligned with the rest of the results. And so on.

In this case, your outliers may show huge gaps in engagement or they may have smaller skews. Treat each outlier as something to consider and review.

Remember: You are going to ignore outliers that do not directly support your Essentialism goal.

I know that ignoring low-scoring items will be difficult at first glance.

Here's an example:

Maybe physical work environment is a category on your survey, and it was scored the lowest overall. And your company is mostly remote with a goal to move to 100% remote over the next two years. Will fixing the physical work environment be helpful to your overall goals? No. Your company is focusing on eliminating the physical work environment (onsite desks) as a whole.

In this example, bettering the work environment was completely disconnected with their Essentialism goal—and definitely not something that would help them achieve their desired results. It's hard to leave a low number on the table, but it will help you as you move along the rest of the action plan steps.

Step 3: Probe Deeper

Now that you have your list of outliers to dig into further, it's time to dig deeper into your results. It's a bit more work than we're currently doing, but this is fun, strategic work and it will have a huge payoff (and you've already limited your digging topics in the previous two steps, so less work overall!).

Results from a company-wide engagement survey are helpful, but they have a ton of biases and skews baked into them. Who participates, who doesn't. Who feels safe answering honestly, who wouldn't for a hundred dollars. And so on.

These results are your starting point, but you want to go deeper. And because we have our Essentialism goal in mind, we're able to go deep in a focused manner, versus being a mile wide and an inch deep (which for the record, doesn't actually influence meaningful change or engagement).

To go deeper, you'll want to do some more one-on-one work, either through focus groups, small staff meetings, lunch and learns (for feedback), and so on—anything that helps you have a direct conversation with employees and leaders, so you can ask more about certain topics without pressure.

Once you've added a few more touchpoints to the survey results, add them to your list, supporting the outlier topics with the additional insight you've captured.

Step 4: Rank

We're finally at the take-action step! This is the fun part because we've done the necessary pre-work that makes this step very easy. Look at our list, which looks something like this:

Essentialism goal
• Outlier list
  ▪ Item 1
    o Supporting insight from conversation
  ▪ Item 2
    o Supporting insight from conversation

Based on your list of outliers, it's time to decide the order of criticality for which you will then start solving. It sounds complicated, but here's exactly what you're going to do: determine which item is the most critical to solve for your Essentialism goal. That this item being low or not aligned or broken, is causing harm—and thus it goes to the top of your list.

Order the rest of your outliers using the same process. Once the most critical one is solved, which is the next critical item? And so on and so forth. This is your plan of attack—the order in which you'll tackle things to increase engagement.

Notice what you're *not* going to do any longer (and we know your managers aren't, either):

- Focus on three key categories to improve over the next year
- Solve your lowest hanging fruit items
- Pick your favorite and go forward

Step 5: Tackle

Because we are being strategic with our engagement factors and action plan, we are starting with *one* thing/outlier to tackle. One thing only. We're going to create our action plan to directly tackle this one thing—and ultimately increase engagement so we can meet our Essentialism goal.

So what goes on this action plan?

You have a lot of information to start with. You know what the question and category is that needs addressing, and you know why employees feel (in their own words) this one thing is so low. Use this information to your advantage.

Your employees have likely shared some solutions and ideas on how to improve the various things you reviewed with them. Consider how these can be turned into action items. We're not looking at the easiest or the quickest results (unless you're being pressured to deliver something quickly); we're looking at the action that will close the gap or eliminate the friction points for your Essentialism goal.

That's your action plan: What will you implement to improve your one thing? Once that is solved and you've measured its success, then—and only then—you move on to your second item.

Your action plan looks vastly different with this approach than it does with our traditional approach. Instead of creating a long list of 1,000 ways to increase engagement and implementing as many as you can, you will be implementing with intentional action—all focused on delivering one specific outcome. Your action plan includes one Essentialism goal, one outlier idea, and one action to address the idea.

With this focused approach, you and your leaders will not only know exactly what to focus on, but you'll also be able to go deep with your one activity to ensure true engagement—which in turn will deliver focused results to your Essentialism goal.

Exit Interviews

When an employee is ready to leave our organization by choice, usually there is a mix of emotions. We are bummed to see an employee go (even more so if they are a top performer), but we also know that people leave organizations for various reasons, and it's something we should expect and plan for. Also, as a fellow human, think back to a job you've exited from. It happens, and it's awkward when you are the person leaving, too.

I can't tell you the number of times I've heard horrible resignation stories (and I've experienced a few myself). Once you've worked up the courage to resign and tell your boss about it, there is a huge relief or weight lifted off your shoulders, coupled with the intent to do great things until you leave. And then you are confronted by the awkwardness. The people you've thought of as your friends don't know how to act around you. You may have been told to not share the news yet with your coworkers, clients, and so forth. People stop talking to you. It's like, in an instant, you have become the office piranha.

Instead of leaving with your positive company experiences intact—because as soon as we have decided to move forward, we want to quickly forget the horribleness—you are left with even more negative experiences and a bad taste in your mouth. Instead of being treated like adults and colleagues, we tend to feel personally slighted when someone resigns, and we let our hurt feelings get in the way of creating a long-lasting, positive experience.

Your former employees are your alumni, and they will *talk*. We discussed in Part II of this book, about your external employee experience, that your alumni and reputation help shape your culture externally. They are the people who will recommend your company to others—or tell them to run the other way. They will consider boomeranging back—or will run toward your competitor. They will share their positive experiences on Glassdoor—or they will put their goodwill aside and share all of the bad things.

And yet, we still don't lead our employees out of the organization in a decent manner. We don't show them respect and kindness for carrying the company torch for however long (or short) they have been with us. We just look at them like they're the next contestant eliminated on *Project Runway* or *The Voice,* and they're out.

This is where exit interviews, at a minimum, combined with common decency, will help your employees transition into alumni gracefully and with their positive employee experiences being the strongest touchpoints. Let's look at this through the Employee Experience Framework.

- Know: what do I need to do to leave on good terms and how do I transition out of the company?

- Feel: relieved to be moving on and excited about what's next, and overall looking back with positivity
- Act: transition knowledge and work efficiently
- Touch: personal touch and then electronic for surveys

Let's get back to exit interviews specifically. These are among the HR activities or campaigns that a lot of us have stopped doing because we didn't find them useful or we felt like people were not being truthful or transparent when we surveyed them in the past.

And that's probably true. We have done a horrible job, as a function, at creating and delivering exit surveys of any value—or, frankly, even caring what happens when someone leaves the organization (because, ahem, they are "no longer our problem"). If we consider the entire experience, though, they become even more important after they leave. They're our ambassadors in the world.

The problem with the many exit interviews I've seen over the years is the questions asked are completely unhelpful—for the employee and for you. They ask broad things like "Why are you leaving the company?"

I remember being asked that question when I was leaving a job, and the response in my head was "Are you kidding me? I have been talking to you for months as to why I'm unhappy—and *now* you care why I'm leaving? Why didn't care then? And also, let me share a list of 16 things that have all added up over time. . . ." What I ended up responding with in the multiple-choice survey was "For other opportunities."

There is absolutely no reason for anyone to share that information with you. Why would they, when you didn't care about it before? And what is a reasonable answer to that, that would have minimal blow-back to the employee? Generally, employees don't want to burn bridges when they leave, and they are approaching these surveys with that mindset.

Some of the other frequent questions that are "suggested" for your survey include these types of questions, with the inner-thought answers that go along with these poorly worded questions:

- Why did you start looking for another job? (When I realized that this place is awful, or my boss is a complete jerk.)
- What does your new position offer that influenced your decision to leave? (More money, more opportunities to advance my career, and flexibility. Oh yeah, and top of the list: It's not HERE.)
- What could we have done better? (Everything? Why are you asking me to do your job for you? I told my boss and HR what the issues were. You never did anything to fix it.)
- Would you ever consider returning to this company? (Dude, at this point, peace.)
- Did you feel that you were equipped to do your job well? (I had to wait six weeks to get the CFO's approval to get a *working laptop.* NO.)
- How would you describe the culture of our company? (Bad.)
- Can you provide more information, such as specific examples? (Nope.)

I kept it clean, but I bet you have thought those same things, or an exiting employee had the guts to say them to you directly, when asked those questions as you were exiting in the organization.

Instead, we need to ask thoughtful questions that keep the framework and employee concerns in mind—while providing us with input that we can take action on. Here are better questions:

Which of our total rewards or benefits did you take most advantage of/use during your time here?
Why this works: It's specific thing with a small scope and a direct question. This allows the employee to move from their feelings about

leaving and focus on something that they used—and you can capture feedback on your total rewards at the same time.

Were there areas in which you felt communication was lacking from senior leadership?
Why this works: It helps you find gaps while at a senior-enough level that they don't feel as connected as they would to their manager.

What was most (or least) helpful piece of feedback you received during your tenure?
Why this works: People remember something that sticks with them, such as helpful or hurtful feedback. This will help you understand feedback norms and the micro culture.

In what ways did you feel that your career aspirations were supported and nurtured during your time here?
Why this works: We ask for specifics regarding what's important for the employee's career aspirations. You'll also get a sense of what's working/broken in L&D.

What leadership skills do you think need improvement at the company?
Why this works: It's not about their direct manager only, but more indicative of their experience and the culture.

What was the most meaningful way you received recognition over the past year?
Why this works: You can drill into the relationship and connection between the employee and the company, and this sheds light into your recognition norms.

These are sample questions that may or may not be applicable to what you need to discover during this phase. To create your own effective exit survey, be sure to start with what you want to find out about. What are your key areas of focus to improve the employee experience? Next, be sure your questions are as open-ended as possible. Text responses are preferred here and will provide you with more applicable information. Finally, make the survey anonymous. That adds an extra layer of comfort for your exiting employee.

A question that comes up next is usually when to have an exiting employee take the exit survey. The answer is, a day or two after they have given their notice. You might want to wait until their last day, and I've even heard of some companies waiting until the employee has exited the organization. Those are terrible ideas. If you deliver the survey while the news is still new, they are still engaged with your company, working toward handing off their work and considering what's next. You want them to be at this stage in the process, not at the end of the awkward or awfulness that they can endure, when there is really zero reason for the employee to share *anything*.

17

COMMUNICATION

YOUR WINNING ADVANTAGE

THE ONE SUCCESS FACTOR THAT DRIVES YOUR EMPLOYEE EXPERIENCE efforts to a roaring success, or derail them on an ongoing basis, is your communication strategy. In 2004, I created my first employee communications department—well before it was "thing"—and have since started and expanded departments at more than 10 big-name companies. Why? Because having expertise in HR isn't enough to frame your employee experiences in a consistently positive light. Instead, we have to relearn how important communications is to *our employees* and make a constant effort to meet them where they are to deliver successful messages.

This is not to say you need to become a communication expert in addition to your current job duties or that you need to hire a consultant to get your employee/HR communications in shape. This section includes some best practices for you to implement to ensure your hard work around the employee experience pays off in the short and long term.

Current State of Employee Communications

"Employee communications" is a fairly new concept—so new that, when I launched my first employee communications department in 2004, the VP of Corporate Communications had absolutely no idea what I would be doing. While official Employee Communications departments or experts may still be emerging, the idea behind this skill set is nothing new.

At the end of the day, employee communication is all about connecting and engaging effectively with your employees and your people. The misconception is that Employee Communications is only focused on how emails get sent out or how we push messages out to our employees. That's a small part of effective communications.

In many companies, Employee Communications is referred to as Internal Communications or Corporate Communications, and is often led by people with a communications or a public relations background rather than HR-based. Because this structure has proven to be ineffective and provides you, a key talent HR professional, with ample opportunity to deliver with impact in the future of HR.

The Need Now—and Going Forward

As HR continues to evolve, being able to effectively connect with your employees will be the difference between a successful HR program and one in which HR is no longer seen as valuable. Making this more difficult are the multigenerational workforce, varied channels to reach your employees, and a usually behind-the-technology-ball workforce that doesn't allow for agile communication change.

While most of these programs can be a serious roadblock when trying to communicate to your employees, it also puts you squarely in the position to shift your employee communications strategy from "communicating at" to "connecting with." And being in HR, there is no one more qualified to make this happen.

As communication technology continues to change, communications written in AP Style or "within corporate brand guidelines" will fail. Messages that are delivered only by email or through leadership cascade will fall on deaf ears. You will be ignoring large pockets of your organization, vastly diminishing your capability to get any work done.

Why This Is a Critical Skill

Employee communications—having your employees feel connected to your company, knowledgeable about what's going on, and engaged around your company's mission—is paramount to every single thing you do in HR each day. When you're able to build relationships with the people you serve, they buy into what HR is delivering. The resistance isn't as strong. It no longer feels like you're yelling into a black hole email after email.

Instead, your employees trust what HR is saying and doing. They're ready to join forces with you to move forward. The HR credibility factor will be the highest it has ever been in the history of HR.

That impact, while focused acutely on internal messaging or HR, does not tell the whole story. When you build a strong rapport/relationship with your people, other groups and senior leaders will be clamoring to understand how you do it. They will want to replicate your success or, likely, ask you to partner with them on projects they deem important—further elevating your skill set, to make a positive impact on the business.

Being able to build relationships, connection, and engagement with your employees will set you apart and elevate your company's success at the same time.

HR Like a Marketer

Having spent most of my time holding dual-roles in HR and Employee Communications, I have always been focused on how to help employees understand what they need to do and why they need to do it, especially when it comes to HR activities. As I've spoken around North America, I have found that *reaching* employees—feeling like HR or leaders are being heard—is an ongoing problem. It's a problem so big that most aren't quite sure where to start.

This leaves a huge gap between what HR wants to do and how we can achieve it. We want to increase employee engagement, so we focus on surveying our employee population to see where things are—then hope leaders implement/address what the results showed.

We want to encourage employees to be healthcare consumers, so we focus on offering new medical plans and benefits that help employees save money and invest wisely—then hope employees figure out what a great investment the company has made and enroll in the right plan for them.

Essentially, we focus on the outcome we want without understanding the core of how to get people there. We know how to create employee engagement surveys, share results, suggest best next steps, and create comprehensive benefits packages, for example. But that's where we stop.

When it comes to sharing the what, how, and why, we either rely on what we did last year (rinse and repeat), slap a communication together haphazardly, or let someone else create a plan/message without really knowing us.

We're letting the most important part of our HR program's success stop short, over and over again—leaving us scratching our heads as to why engagement didn't really improve or why people still aren't enrolling in that new, high-deductible healthcare plan.

Communicating to your employees in a strategic and thoughtful way is the only way to create a connection with them. With connection comes engagement. With engagement come positive actions and outcomes. Instead of focusing solely on the HR activity, it's necessary to focus on how you are telling your employees about the HR activity.

Think of our friends in Marketing. They spend a lot of time considering who their perfect "buyer" is. They create avatars, find their niche, target their market, hang out where they are, create a story, and continuously reinforce their brand (and brand promise). Why aren't we doing that too for HR or leaders?

The easy answer is, it's hard and well outside of most of our wheelhouses. It is an actual skill—and you have a job with responsibilities and your own deliverables.

But what if I told you that there is a simple process that's repeatable for you to instantly up-level your communications? To gain back all of the communication credibility that your HR department or senior leadership team has lost and create better communications? There is: my HRLAM (HR Like a Marketer) Thread.

This process is used when you are writing the actual communications you want to share with employees. The channel of delivery (email, snail mail, newsletter, text message, etc.) isn't important for now. This is the "pen to paper" content creation to support your employee experience programs to success.

For each communication, you begin by outlining what success looks like for the:

- Campaign: the project
- Message: the individual communication
- Action items: what steps employees need to take to complete the action

This is a quick inventory to keep you tied to the purpose of the activity and the communication. Remember: We are always going to keep our Employee Experience Framework at the top of each project so we're constantly tying back to our overall goals.

For the communication writing itself, let's pull the thread!

HRLAM Thread

| Change | Connection | Barrier | Conquer | CTA |

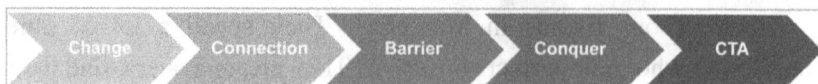

Each communication will walk through these five steps to ensure you're crafting an effective message. After practicing the process a few times, you'll find yourself analyzing your emails, texts to friends, and more through the HRLAM lens. Here's the thread broken down at a high level.

Change
What does your employee need to "overcome"? What is the mindset shift you are asking them to make?

Employees are coming to the table at a certain point in time, with their own knowledge base and experience. In order to be successful in the project or activity, what shift in perspective needs to happen?

Connection
What does the employee you want to communicate to/care about? What's in it for them?

Sound familiar? In order to create a connection in our communications, we have to clearly share why they care about what we're saying.

For example, if you are telling employees your employee engagement survey is open, include how the results are going to be used, who's going to take action on the input and when, and so forth—in other words, why it's worth their effort.

Barrier

What is standing in their way? Or, what is keeping them from succeeding with your request right now? What knowledge do they need?

Think back to the bridge analogy from earlier in the book. The same idea applies here. What is currently preventing your employee from completing action, and what do they need to know to hit submit (aka walk across the bridge)?

Conquer

Once they overcome the barrier, what does success look like? If I cared about what you're telling me, I get this result/outcome. Share the "other side of the coin."

Nothing feels as good as success, so share the future vision with employees. Granted, most work-related success outcomes aren't crazy outlandish, but they are meaningful. And who says you can't have more fun with this?

For example, if you're communicating about annual enrollment and benefit offerings, share how comforted an employee will feel once they enroll or a story about how benefits have helped a colleague's family member.

CTA (Call to Action)

What *one* action do you want your employee to take after reading/interacting with your message?

Back to "one thing": It's an important theme. Why? Well, consider receiving an email for benefits enrollment and the email was two pages long with 10 different links and steps for you to take to complete enrollment. You start out confident, clicking the first link, which takes you to an external website where you have to complete some information. Oops, then you have a scheduled meeting and your progress in the email is lost. Do you go back to your inbox an additional nine times in between your other work to keep completing tasks, or do you pick up the phone and call the benefits center?

When we have too many action items to take, we get frozen in overwhelm and don't know how to move forward. Especially when it's an action item or outcome that we care deeply about. So use only *one* CTA: go here and do this. If there's another step, communicate it at that point, or create a landing page where you send employees, and they can self-select the step they are at.

Go to bettHR.com/hrlam to download the HRLAM quick-wins workbook.

Senior Leadership Communications

All employee-facing communications are important when creating your ideal employee experience, but your senior leadership communications carry extra weight. Why? Because employees look to their senior leaders to set the tone, focus areas of what's important, and a stated level of expectations.

Companies and senior leaders themselves go about crafting communications in various ways. Sometimes it's written by the leader or by Corporate Communications or by the department sharing the update, and so on. Depending on the weight of the content the message carries, it can be reviewed by several departments and experts (Legal, Marketing, HR, etc.) before it's shared with employees. And when it is, it's bland, boring, and in corporate branding style (i.e., AP style), and it lacks transparency and weight.

Not all communications are written this way, but most are. Ever notice why the CEO emails that go viral are the ones that contain something transparent, honest, and people-relatable? It's because so few of these messages are seen by employees.

Ideally, your senior leaders will communicate using the HRLAM process or reach out to you for guidance. Because we can't rely on that, here are some ways you can help ensure these messages are *helpful* and track toward supporting your employee experience, versus creating a negative impact.

First, help them understand your employee experience goals by sharing your framework (macro or micro, depending on the communication). From there, help them define what you need them to cover or say—the "what's important for the employee." And finally, provide them with one easy CTA.

If you present this in an easy-to-absorb format, it will be seen as helpful and time-saving for your senior leader (versus overly directive or offensive).

Here's an example:

> Hi Senior Leader,
> To follow up from our discussion, here is some information to make it easy for you to craft the message launching the employee engagement survey. Let me know if I can help at all!

The employee experience we want to reinforce:

Know: Why should I bother taking my time to do this and will anything be done with the results?
Answer: As the most valuable investment to our company, we take your feedback seriously. Once the survey closes on July 31, we will compile the data and share the company-level feedback during our quarterly town hall on Sept. 1. Each manager will receive specific feedback the following day and will be sharing that with you before Sept. 15.

Feel: Open to sharing their feedback and safe that it will be received anonymously/constructively.

Answer: This survey is done through a third party and is fully anonymous. They will be doing a second anonymization of the results before compiling and sharing it with us. Your feedback is anonymous, and we are eager to hear it.

Act: Complete the survey intentionally.

Answer: Click here to share your feedback with us.

Touch: Online link that can anonymize participants.

———

In a nutshell, insert your key messages or bullet points into the appropriate category to help guide the message creation.

One final note about your senior leadership communications: Cadence and frequency matter.

At a previous company where I worked, we had a new leader who missed the memo on how important it is to actually connect and communicate with all of the employees under her. Her first directors and above meeting with her team didn't take place until six months into her tenure. Her first all-employee town hall, in which she only provided the opening and closing remarks, took place nine months into her tenure. Needless to say, she was not an employee favorite.

Help your senior leaders set up an ongoing communication plan that includes various ways and touchpoints for them to interact with their employees. Town halls are great—even better if the format resembles a traditional town hall, where the audience is able to stand up and ask questions directly. Regardless of the channel, frequency matters. Employees want to hear from their senior leaders. These communications reinforce the employee experience and reaffirm to employees that their mission still matters.

Communication Tactics and Channels

How you communicate is through communication tactics, and the delivery is through channels. At work, most of communication channels include email, instant messaging, home mailing, social forum (like Yammer), intranet, chatbot, town halls, audio, video, text messaging, site slides, posters, table tents, and more. The list is endless and forever changing.

Being intentional with how and where you communicate is an important delivery tactic when creating your employee experience— particularly in the touchpoint section. However, taking a moment to consider the channel and audience before you communicate, whether it be a project message or a personal work message, will help your communications be more effective.

One of the things I hear often from employees and leaders alike is that "people don't read emails"—that inboxes are so cluttered nowadays, and that's why employees aren't taking action, reading, or following up.

That couldn't be further from the truth. The problem isn't the channel delivery: It's with your communication credibility and the message. And perhaps the message isn't right for the channel you've chosen.

By default, most of us spend a majority of our days in our email inbox. And yes, we all get more than enough emails—but I guarantee you read every email from someone you deem credible and important. The CFO shares a financial update and whether or not there will be layoffs? You definitely open that one. Your boss sends something urgent? You're taking a peek.

The point is, the more credible a communicator you are—and the more appropriately matched your channel is—the more effective your communication will be.

Consider the CFO email again. Would that be as effective if they instant messaged you? Or perhaps sent a short text?

To increase your communication credibility, follow the HRLAM principles. It will help your message be focused, *helpful,* and *informative* to your audience.

To better understand channels, we first have to understand why communicating through different channels is important.

Think about the ways in which you learn best. It is by reading, seeing, hearing, touching, or interacting? Or perhaps a combination of a few of these? When we create learning programs, we now consider how to deliver the message in a few ways. We add closed captioning for those who need to read or an audio-only download if visual is not preferred, and so on.

Most of us are not considering the same knowledge/learning factor when we craft communications and content to support a project. And because of this, we are never going to reach employees who learn differently than the channel we're providing for them. Information is not a one-size-fits-all solution, so if your current communications are sent as they always have been (ahem, email or home mail only), then you are putting a big ding in your employee experience.

Take me, for example. I am not an auditory learner. In fact, even on phone calls, I need to be doing something actively with my hands to be sure I'm engaging the right brain muscles to pay attention to what's being said. (If you know me well enough, you know that means I'm playing Spider Solitaire at all times when on a call.)

As you consider each communication and message that touches your employee experience, be sure you're considering the most effective channel (or channels!) to deliver that message. That doesn't mean that you have to create multiple communications for a single message. It means that you repurpose your one HRLAM content message and deliver it in a few ways.

Let's use that CFO email once more. If we believe that an email is the best method, let's craft the message using the HRLAM technique to ensure it's effective and it ties back to the employee experience goals. Once that communication is ready, consider additional channels. At a minimum, an audio recording or the CFO reading the email could be helpful. A video is another great idea (suspend "How do I do this?" for a moment). Posting an interactive article on the intranet would be another touchpoint. And so on.

Using the one piece of content, you repurpose it for different channels—and then share, with options. If you do this for the most important messages, your employees will appreciate the effort and be able to choose the best way to learn for them—putting your employee back as the hero of the story.

Go to bettHR.com/repurpose to learn about the tools we use to repurpose content on a budget.

18

METRICS FOR YOUR COMMUNICATIONS

THE IMPORTANCE OF CREATING METRICS CANNOT BE OVERSTATED. IT'S the only way we can know that the work we're doing is adding any value. It helps us decide what to spend our time and money on. And it helps you justify a change of direction, a new idea, highlighting attention, and so on.

But metrics can feel overwhelming to many of us. If you're not a math expert, it can feel like a mountain not worth trying to climb. That's a myth! Metrics is just a component to how we frame a story around the work we do.

Metrics is the quickest way for you to establish yourself as a strategic partner and superstar, especially in our current work environment and with the changes happening in the marketplace. As we move forward, tactical duties will be fulfilled by AI, and leaders who are able to be strategic will continue to drive value to the organization.

Don't worry: We won't get into the nitty gritty numbers here, but understand that, by using metrics in the work we do—particularly around the employee experience—you are adding *additional* strategic value and influence in your organization.

When you focus on a big project such as the employee experience, you have to know what what's working and what's not in order to adjust or keep things moving forward. Here are some best practices and ideas to help you get started with metrics in a non-scary way.

There isn't a perfect starting place with HR metrics. There's isn't a "best practice" that is the absolute answer—which is a good thing! But there are metrics to be found, created, and tracked, for every single activity you do. (Don't try to start tracking them all at once, or your entire world will be all about the metrics, forgetting about the work.)

I have a few reliable standard metrics, that I suggest you start with —or at least start thinking about first. Remember that what makes metrics work, is the uniqueness of them, specific to your business and practice, and the goals within your employee experience you are trying to achieve.

Since we're talking about communications, let's start with email communication metrics.

Tracking metrics around every single employee-facing email communication you send is a great place to start. Yes, I am a bit biased since I'm a communicator, but it is also the most direct contact you have with your employees. Thus, this action is capable of creating the biggest impact to the work you do.

I get push-back on the "every single" email thing, usually with responses like "But it's just a reminder email" or "We don't really have an action for our employees to take from this message." We have already tackled those fallacies in the HRLAM section. If you are communicating with your employees, there needs to be a point.

Start putting metrics around your messages. How often are you emailing employees? Can you track how many messages a typical employee inbox is getting from you (and, bonus, all other corporate functions) within a day/week/month? Of course, you have open rates, click-through rates, and bounce rates to check out—but start with the metrics you have access to first.

The next set of suggested metrics are behavior-driven.

Start looking at various actions and behaviors your employees are taking. You can look through various lenses: benefits enrollments, multimedia watches/opens, call center activities, performance plans, intranets, responses, completed actions, and so on. Essentially, what are your employees doing or not doing? Create metrics around that.

For example, if you are trying to increase your HR department's efficiency and impact, knowing what your employees are actually spending their time on can greatly impact how you want to spend your time. Are they taking the actions you want (or need) them to take? Are they aware of a specific offering or program? Do they know where to go to ask questions?

Start with an employee behavior that matters to your leadership team and your employee experience, and show them how it's working. Use these types of metrics to reinforce your deliverables—not the other way around.

The idea is to just *start*. Start capturing data around the work you do. Look at your inbox to see how many questions (and the types of questions) you get. Is turnover critical to achieve your experience plans? Then track that. Start with what's easy and accessible, and then grow your metrics scope from there.

Go to bettHR.com/hrm101 to learn more about implementing metrics.

Creating an effective internal employee experience strategy is the quickest way for you to build a positive relationship and connection with your employees. Doing so leads to higher engagement, innovation, and buy-in. And while the other parts of the experience (macro, external, and leader) are important, the internal experience is the most urgent with the most immediate results.

It also ensures the work that you show up to do adds value in the right way to your company's goals and bottom line—and helps you stay motivated as an employee yourself, by providing you with meaningful work with visible change.

Yet, at the same time, changing the internal employee experience takes time. And it can feel like an uphill battle to try to make such a big change companywide. Change happens by each individual, not all at once, so focus on one employee's experience. Narrow it down to improving the life of that one person. If you're not sure who to choose, remember that you are an employee too. You deserve to show up to work and feel valued, appreciated, and encouraged to succeed at each step of the way while doing work that is strategic and keeps *you* motivated and connected.

The internal employee experience is so much more than how we've approached engagement activities. It's not a gimmick or throwing hundreds of things out there and hoping something resonates. It's about being intentional in our interactions to build a connection, measuring what's working and what needs adjusting, being consistent, and being transparent. If we do these things, we can create positive experiences for employees to put in their bank. With enough of these, the negative blips that will always be there when working with people can be canceled out and overcome.

To learn more about how to implement the strategies and tactics we've reviewed in this section, go to bettHR.com/metrics.

IV

THE LEADER'S EMPLOYEE EXPERIENCE

As a leader in an organization, you have been given enormous responsibility to ensure the success of your people, their deliverables, the department, and your company. And in most companies, the weight of leadership—of good and effective leadership—isn't valued or nurtured. Most of the time we hire or promote a leader and let them lead with minimal (if any) training and very little support or guidelines on how to lead toward a common goal. This approach often leads to leadership issues or outright failures, and we can't really fault a specific person or thing.

The truth is, all leaders—even seasoned ones—need a framework to not only manage, but also how to lead by cultivating experiences and building connections. While we won't focus on leadership "advice" or the top characteristics of a "good" leader here, what we review in this section will help you become a *more effective* leader and a *better team builder.*

This is true whether you are leading a large team or a team of one, or you are practicing self-leadership. The employee experience framework will help you show up as a leader, without wasting time and energy on things that don't match your style or goals. Ready?

19

LEADER'S EMPLOYEE EXPERIENCE FRAMEWORK

BEING AN EMPLOYEE EXPERIENCE-FOCUSED LEADER MEANS THAT YOUR approach of overall leadership (not management!) is focused on building momentum with your team, toward the ideal experience. We do this by thinking of our team members as our customers—with you, the leader, as the guide and your team members, the hero.

When I reflect on the leaders I enjoyed working with the most, there wasn't a difference of expectations or standards between how they interacted with our external clients and with their internal team. They brought the same type of focus with the same approach, regardless whether person was external or internal.

Conversely, the leaders that I had the most friction with led in a way that caused power struggles all over the place. In general, they led from a place of insecurity or superiority instead of a place of collaboration. The way they spoke and interacted with our clients was from a place of respect, partnership, and "the customer is always right." Internally, their approach was from a place of "I'm right," "Do it as I've asked," or "You're my minions and I'll take the credit."

While growing into a more effective leader will take time and practice, implementing this framework will help you expand your skills, reinforce your vision, and build (or rebuild if needed) your relationship with your team.

Know

Just like you would approach a micro experience or project, the Know factor will vary based on what you're trying to convey and communicate. The critical components for Know are:

1. Remember that you are the guide and your team members are the hero. By guiding them along their journey, they instantly care more about what you are saying because it's framed in a way that matters most to them.
2. Be specific and transparent in what your team needs to know—and what they need.
3. Do not be ambiguous. With a lack of knowledge and information, your team will create their own story, which will likely be worse than the actual situation.
4. Tie the information back to the experience and company goals.

As a leader, there are several very real boundaries that your company requires you to uphold. Those boundaries are important, and I wouldn't advise you to cross over the line. But there is a way to deliver information or hold information back until it's the appropriate time, without coming across as a jerk, fake, or the dreaded corporate drone/company man. By going down this path, your team will stop listening to and you will lose respect in your leadership.

In so many situations over the years I've had to withhold company confidential information to my team or share information that I didn't agree with. It's not an easy place to be in, but it's a big part of being a people leader.

To get around or through these situations, be a person—and communicate the information in a way that you would like to receive it. For example, while it was forever frustrating (to the point it was a punchline for my peers), one of my favorite bosses used the phrase *company steward* whenever he was sharing tough news. It was his way of reminding us that, our personal feelings aside, we had to deliver some company-related news as a responsible leader in the organization.

How we then package the news to our team and share that knowledge are what's important as a leader. If you refer to these considerations within the framework, you will be able to deliver good and bad news, updates, projects, and so forth, with each employee still connected to the desired outcome we want to reinforce (and they want to experience).

Feel

If you have an aversion to feelings like I do, you'll find that being a leader and having to dig into the Feel part of what you're conveying can be the most difficult step, mainly because each team member will come to the news/update/knowledge with their own perspective and emotional scale. This is a variable, and, as leaders, we're expected to be able to handle most emotions our employees exhibit.

Generally, when sharing an update, leading a meeting, having a one-on-one, and so on, you want to be very clear and specific about the type of feeling and emotion(s) you want to evoke. With intention, you will be able to more effectively influence your own positioning, which will help your team follow your lead.

Let me share an example, which I have unfortunately had to carry out lots of times over my career. Most leaders dread (and don't always agree with) this action: laying off or firing employees.

It is never an easy thing to choose or deliver the news that one of your team members is not going to have continued employment—regardless of the reason. But it is a part of being a leader and a manager that most will have to address during their career.

Before I go into an employee release conversation, I do a quick, four-bullet outline of the experience. For Feel, my bullet reads "respected as a person; graceful exit."

That is the ideal emotion I want an employee to feel during the exit conversation. With that intention, I am able to create a script and review the process and materials to have that kind of conversation. Granted, it's a very short conversation, and there are best practices as to what to say and not to say, but I create an environment in which my goal is to help the employee leave with respect and grace. About 85% of the time, that's the emotion that the employee feels because I've been intentional. The other 15% of the time, I wouldn't have been able to effectively influence their emotions more than I did (for various reasons). Overall, I'm pleased with that outcome, especially for such a difficult activity for all those involved.

This same emotion-check should be predetermined before your employee interactions—not so it's formulaic, but so you gut-check your own approach and better set up your team and you for a successful interaction and experience. Have a difficult email to write? What emotion do you want to evoke to encourage action? (Hint: It's usually not the emotion that comes through an angry tirade response.)

Simple framing, language usage, and taking a moment to pick an emotion will greatly change your communication style and influence for the better.

Act

Helping your team members know exactly what to do next can quickly move you into the dreaded micromanaging realm, which we all want to stay as far away from as possible. Nothing good comes from micromanagement when it comes to the employee experience.

However, you *do* want to consider the next best action—without telling the team *how* to get that action done. Do you see the difference?

People feel micromanaged when they are not only told what but also how. When you're evaluating the next best action, think of it in terms of outcome: What needs to be achieved or completed? *That* is the Act you want to reinforce.

Holding back the second part of that—the how—can be difficult to get used to, but trust your team to ask you *how* if they need that support. Providing them with a clear action and outcome will provide them with the success factor on their hero journey, while letting them choose their own path—reinforcing their own skills and knowledge base.

For example, let's say you need your team to have performance management ratings in by a certain date. Your action be something along the lines of "Be sure to send along your ratings worksheet to me no later than close of business next Friday [use the actual date]." That's the action. What you're not going to do is then provide them with the process on how to get that worksheet done—unless it's a best practice training. Basically, unlike all of the math tests we took in school, we don't need our team to show us their work, as long as they complete the action.

Touch

As a leader, the touchpoints available to us are usually determined by others in the organization. Therefore, you have a specific set of tools and touchpoints to communicate and interact with your team to choose from.

Here's the quickest trick to ensure your touchpoints are effective. Ask each team member the following:

- How do you best like to be communicated to? Is there a difference if it's critical or urgent?
- What is your least favorite communication channel?
- How do prefer to be recognized?
- What kind of feedback works best for you?

These questions will remove the ambiguity around which

touchpoints to use. And if you create a mini-bio for each team member to keep handy and build on, you can always be sure to get this part of the puzzle right.

The hardest part about this approach is that each team member may have a different preference, and it's not efficient to be re-communicating things multiple ways. Instead, what you'll agree upon with your entire team is a guiding practice. Here's one many of our clients use: As a team, we agree to share team-wide information and updates via email and/or during our weekly leadership meetings. For individual feedback, focus areas, action items, and so forth, we will communicate according to the agreed-upon communication channels.

This helps you choose one or two (email and meetings) broad messaging touchpoints and also allows for customization and personalization for individual needs. Remember that employees learn and process information differently. By communicating according to your overlapping touchpoint preferences, your team member will feel heard and seen, creating a very positive experience.

20

YOUR LEADERSHIP INFLUENCE AND CAPABILITIES

EARLY IN MY CAREER, I WORKED WITH A LEADER WHO HAD A WOODEN sign hanging on his office wall that said, "It is what it is." As a young, type-A, ambitious employee, the sign rubbed me the wrong way every time I saw it. Finally, I asked him why he had it up there and what it meant to him.

His answer surprised me: to remind him and his team members to focus on the things that they can influence—and to let everything else go. This was well before Elsa started preaching for all of us to "let it go," but it was a similar concept. Instead of it being a negative thing— something that I equated to shrugging your shoulders and giving up—it was the complete opposite within his leadership sphere. It focused his and his team's energy on the activities that were worth their effort, instead of everything at once.

At the same company, one of my leaders used to call out, "Gravity issue" during meetings. He had a similar mindset: Just like you can't change the pull of gravity, there are just some things at this company and in your job that you just can't change. Those things are gravity issues and are to be ignored or forgotten.

As a leader, being able to identify what is within your area of influence, and what's not, will save you a lot of time and energy, not to mention frustration and early burnout. The same goes for your team members.

If you're able to set the proper boundaries around expectations, the work, deliverables, and so on, you can focus on the activities that directly influence the employee experience. And if the work you do adds value to the experience, you are strengthening the bond and connection—true engagement.

In the same vein, as we've discussed throughout this book, there are going to be *a lot* of decisions, choices, procedures, and so forth that will be outside of your decision-making influence. Perhaps most of them will not be the same the decision you would have made, and others may irk the devil out of you, but they are gravity issues. If you don't have the decision-making power to change the thing that's in your way or the system that is being used, work within what you *can* influence.

Learning how to reframe this perspective within your own experiences and leadership expectations, and then teaching your team how to do the same, will remove many of the barriers they run into during their time at the company. It also leads you to achieve more, since you're able to focus more narrowly.

In addition to your scope of influence, your leadership capabilities are an important piece of the leader's employee experience agenda. In a dream world in which all leaders are created equal and emerge into leadership as fully formed, outstanding people leaders, this wouldn't be a consideration. But I have yet to see that world or meet anyone who has hatched with those skills.

The reality is, we all have our own strengths and weaknesses, including with our own leadership development. As part of this process, critical self-awareness about these areas will help you move forward—not only as you develop your own leadership skills by practicing the right muscles, but also as you grow your team member's leadership skills. An effective leader helps their team become better leaders in their own right.

This reality check is also where you set yourself and your team up for success, by having people with different skills, backgrounds, education, life experiences, ages, genders, and so on around you, to create innovative thought and discussion. When you consider your role as a leader responsible for building and/or reinforcing the ideal employee experience for your team, you can't do that if you aren't able to expand everyone's perspectives.

Diversity and inclusion is a hot topic in HR departments right now —and that's well overdue. We're not going to dive deep into diversity as a whole here, but know it's a very important piece of the experience puzzle and how you succeed as a leader.

Your employee population is made of individuals who have all lived unique lives, with so many pieces adding to the overall puzzle of who they are as people. They are then expected to show up as the unique people they are in a work environment, to varying degrees of welcome, acceptance, inclusion, participation, and more. Your role is to make them feel welcomed and encouraged—and to ensure through your hiring practices (at a minimum) that you continue to create a culture of community.

The comfortable thing to do is to hire for skills or personalities that are most like you. It's that little spark you get when you're interviewing someone for a role and you think, "That person reminds me of me" or "I really like them." That's not always a bad thing, but it's definitely not always the right thing when considering candidates. Hire for the gaps. Hire for a missing perspective on your team. Hire for experience in a different industry. Hire to craft the *best* team, not a comfortable one for you.

As a leader, people with different backgrounds and experiences are not just "diverse." They encourage diverse thought, conversations, new perspectives, and more. To lead the experience, you want to lead a diverse experience that is inclusive of all. Otherwise, all of the hard work you're doing as a leader and the flag-carrier for the employee experience will be doing more harm than good.

21

LET'S FIX IT: LEADERS!

As a leader, you arguably have the most influence over shaping your employee's experience. Being intentional with how you apply the framework will make your job easier—and your employees more engaged. As was the case in the Let's Fix It: HR! Chapter, the solutions presented here are compiled from best practices across the companies we've worked with and have shown great results. They aren't ideas or theories; they are actionable solutions to help you be the best leader you can be.

Ready?

Let's fix it, then.

Creating Your Blueprint

Early in my career, I was responsible for creating communication campaign blueprints, one-page documents that outlined the campaign's goals and the blueprint of how we'd get there. Since then, I've used blueprints for everything, and I suggest you consider creating your team's as well.

Here's an example blueprint template.

	Start Date **Current State**	Focus Area 1	Focus Area 2	Focus Area 3	Focus Area 4	End Date **Future State**
Stated culture/employee experience statement	Capture the friction points, gaps, and success areas to clearly define where you are starting	• How you are going to achieve this, as related to this focus area • Create specific milestones and deliverables (1-3)	• How you are going to achieve this, as related to this focus area • Create specific milestones and deliverables (1-3)	• How you are going to achieve this, as related to this focus area • Create specific milestones and deliverables (1-3)	• How you are going to achieve this, as related to this focus area • Create specific milestones and deliverables (1-3)	Detail how your employee experience will be different at the end date. This is the ideal state. To achieve this, each focus area needs to contribute to the overall result—you are not able to reach this future state, without success in each focus area.

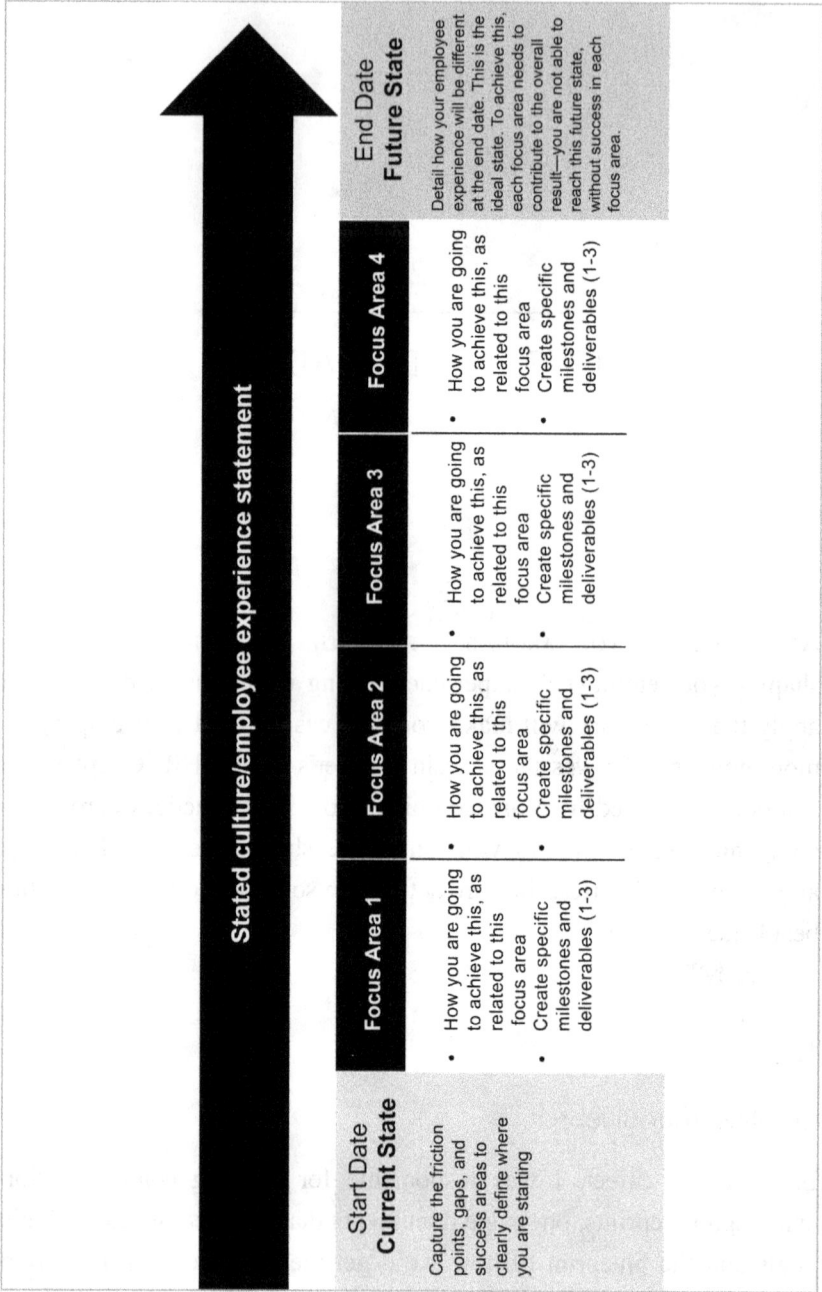

Figure: Blueprint Template

The purpose of your team's blueprint is to share the stated culture/experience statement at the top, to ensure all activities are reinforcing success there. Then, you document where you are right now—the starting point or current state. This section includes things that are working well or that need some attention. And the next step is to create the future state or point of arrival. What will the team or experience look and feel like, once you've achieved success (or reach the end of the year)?

The items that fall in between those two states are the meat of the blueprint. These are the high-level focus areas of *how* you are going to get there. They're the three or four buckets or topics that your team should focus on—with some milestones to mark off along the way.

The blueprint, which you will work on with your direct reports to define and refine, is then used as a measurement of success and a gut-check point for projects that come up that were unexpected. We ask, "Do we do this shiny new project? What does the blueprint say?"— always reinforcing the overall experience goals and providing your team a set of guidelines and determining factors to help them make difficult decisions.

Communication Cadence

We've already reviewed why communicating in different channels and by each employee's preferences is important, but in addition to that, there are ongoing communication principles that can help you build connection over time. This means ongoing two-way communications with your team members. At each communication moment, focus on the framework points (Know, Feel, Act, Touch) to ensure the message is received as intended.

The Ideal Leadership Calendar

We are going to build out the ideal leadership calendar from the individual on up. Depending on what you're currently doing, it may feel overwhelming or impossible. Start by adding in the below new touchpoints one at a time, as you get more comfortable with the practice. The goal here is to create a collaborative environment in which your team feels heard, listened to, in the loop, and supported. That can take a lot of communication—especially if there's been a gaping void in the past.

One-on-One Meetings

Schedule a recurring, 30-minute meeting, at least every other week, with each of your direct reports. This meeting should follow the same formula each time:

1. Macro experience or goal
2. Urgent items that need to be discussed or direction provided
3. Updates, knowledge-sharing, things to keep an eye on
4. Team member updates (excellent/poor performance, issues, feedback, etc.)
5. Company updates
6. Open discussion

By providing your direct reports with a consistent, ongoing, and reliable meeting time, along with the agenda format, they will come to the meeting prepared and keep non-urgent matters off your desk. The key here is to foster two-way communication. And really, is there anything worse than a one-on-one meeting that ends up being a waste of time because there are no updates to share or no discussion to be had?

The ideal format for these would be in-person or, if you are on a virtual team, via video chat. (Yes, it's annoying to get used to being on video, but it adds a very important visual cue for both of you and creates a personal connection, bad hair days and all.)

A quick note about meetings: Meetings get a bad rap because we have become terrible meeting leaders and attendees. They are only effective if you walk into the meeting knowing exactly what will be discussed, what needs to be decided, and what the next action is—and, of course, having the right people in the room, without any non-essential attendees. Here's your reminder to visit your meeting philosophy as a whole, start declining (the world won't end) if you're not truly needed, and start asking for agendas and decision points, before you attend.

Skip-Level Meetings

A skip-level meeting is where you, as the leader, meet one-on-one with the people who report to your direct reports. You skip a level (your direct reports) and have a one-on-one with the employees reporting to your direct reports. I don't know why most leaders don't have these meetings, but they are more than worth the time and effort. You will learn a lot of information about how the organization is *actually* working, and get a pulse on topics, ideas, and culture, all while building connections and providing a safe space for discussion. In addition, you get exposure to team members you likely don't interact with as much—and vice versa.

You should hold 30-minute one-on-one skip-level meetings at least twice per year—or quarterly if you're able. The agenda for this meeting is a bit different: It's up to the skipped level to bring their own agenda to the table. If that seems to open-ended or scary for some of your team members, you can provide some questions or project topics that you want to discuss, but essentially, this meeting should be all about what they want to "bubble up" to you.

Scheduling these could be an absolute nightmare depending on your team size, so I recommend using an online scheduling software like Calendly or Acuity to have the employees you are meeting with choose a time that works for both of your schedules, without the mess of going back and forth.

Direct Report Leadership Meetings

This meeting is for all employees who report to you to come together as a team in a meeting led by you. Usually these are an hour in length and are held at least every other week.

The goal of these meetings is for you to provide focus, clarity, and updates (company, team, and projects); share news, have open discussion; and—perhaps most important—have your team members get to be teammates. This meeting is more about action: what's going on, what needs to happen, what you need to know right now, and so on.

All-Team Meetings

All-team meetings are sometimes referred to as town halls or all-hands meetings, but the premise is the same: Everyone who reports up to you joins one meeting, usually via web conferencing software if employees are scattered across the country/world or virtual.

During this meeting, you can change the agenda, flow, and purpose as needed, but be sure you include an open forum or Q&A (like an actual town hall), provide meaningful updates that track toward the experience, and recognize employees for accomplishments.

I have found these to be well-received when held monthly, but at a minimum every other month works well. Try very hard to resist the normalized cadence in the marketplace of only holding them quarterly or even less frequently. The more your team hears from you, the better.

Talent Management Reviews

This is an item that is usually managed by HR, but that doesn't mean it's not something you can (and should!) be doing. Talent management reviews are meetings when your direct reports come together to review the talent in your organization.

There are a lot of components to having a good talent management meeting, but once you've done it once, it's easy to continue it on an ongoing basis. We won't dive deep into the details here, but if you want to know how to hold these meetings, go to bettHR.com/tmr.

These should be held at least annually, as they do take a lot of time to review all team members, but they provide a better sense of your talent pool. You will be able to better support your key talent if you do them twice per year.

Other Meetings to Consider

I don't think you need to add a ton of additional meetings to your already-busy calendar, but here are some other meetings to consider based on your company culture.

- Daily huddles: This is a quick meeting at the start of the day to review key priorities and any urgent updates. It usually takes less than 15 minutes and sets the tone and expectations daily. These tend to work best on smaller teams or in manufacturing departments.
- All-leadership meetings: In addition to your direct reports, you would have an ongoing meeting with all people leaders who report up to you. The content and tone for this meeting are more closely aligned with the all-employee meetings but focused on more leader-driven updates and decisions. These are especially helpful when you want to reinforce your Employee Experience Framework or are rolling out a new project and want to gain some community and collaboration.
- Key talent calls: These are structured the same as skip-level meetings, but the employee you meet with is different. Instead of one level below your direct report, the employee can be at any level—but they have been identified as key talent. You want to have them lead the discussion, and recognize and encourage their talent and growth.

Be the Coach

You know that being a leader and being a manager are two very different things. As a leader, you encourage your team, help them grow their own skills, provide positive and negative feedback, hear and integrate differing viewpoints, and inspire people to follow your vision. As a manager or a boss, you coordinate and direct activities and team members to deliver what's needed; it's more directive.

Both approaches can be effective, but from the employee experience perspective, leading will beget more positive touchpoints while building in more self-starting and thought leadership by your team members. Think of it in the same vein as the as the proverb *Give a person a fish, and you feed them for a day. Teach a person to fish, and you feed them for a lifetime.* From a leadership perspective, a manager gives a fish, whereas a leader teaches a person to fish. Wouldn't you rather have a team filled with people who can fish on their own?

Learning how to be a coach for your employees is one of the best skills you can invest in for yourself—and for your team. Fair warning: It's one that you need to practice getting used to. The premise of coaching your team is to be available to them as a resource and be great at asking powerful questions.

It starts with how you arrive and show up mentally to a conversation. This is where you, as the leader, have to remember the Employee Experience Framework for the project or conversation, to be aligned with the emotion you want to evoke, not the emotion you may be feeling at the moment. From there, it's about you being *open* to listening and asking questions.

Here are some things for you to consider bringing into your coaching conversations going forward. (I have these written out on a notecard that's in front of me at all times, to remind me to coach, not tell.)

Ask Open-Ended Questions

This takes a slight pause before you ask a question, but you can ask the same thing just framed slightly differently. For example, "Do you have any other options?" is a closed question. The only response is *yes* or *no*. By reframing the question to "What other options do you have?" you have opened up the types of responses.

Open-ended questions are key to not only encouraging more conversation, but they also change the mindset of your employee and keep them talking through the situation. Many times, a closed question could trigger a defensive response or put your employee in a place of feeling as though they've overlooked the obvious answer, whereas an open-ended question asks your employee to use their critical-thinking skills to work out the problem, out loud and in collaboration with you.

"Tell Me More. . . ."

One of my friends is a masterful coach, and the one phrase she says more than any other is, "You mentioned that (fill in the blank). Tell me more about that." *Tell me more* is a genius three-word pairing. Use it as frequently as possible.

It works so well because you're asking for more (details, background, solutions, etc.) and moving the conversation forward, where solutions or new nuggets of information will magically appear. This is particularly helpful when your employee is trying to solve a problem that isn't obvious—or when they've brought a false problem to the table, hoping you uncover the underlying problem. When you ask for more, you can continue to investigate without being too pointed or directive.

Stop Leading to Your Outcome

When you're coaching, you don't want to be a teller; you want your employee to collaborate with you or come up with the solution as an outcome of your discussion. Often, we ask questions that will help lead our employee to what *we* think is the best solution or option or way forward. That isn't being a great coach; that's giving them a fish! Ask for variables and work through them together instead.

Stop Asking Why

Digging into the why of things is one of the quickest ways to get your conversation off track. I know, for my fellow curious leaders out there, it's *hard*. But when you ask *why*, the person on the other end of that question is left defending their motivation or questioning their decision-making skills. Neither of those is a good thing, especially when you're trying to have a productive conversation.

Instead, with a slight rephrasing, you can still find out the why, but by asking *what* questions.

Here's an example:

- No: Why did you miss the deadline?
- Yes: What factors led to you missing the deadline?

See how easy that is? Think through these two questions regarding a missed deadline. *Why* indicates that you failed, whereas *what* provides you some room for explanation and discussion.

There are many other skills to become a great coach, but these question-reframes will help get you started.

Recognition

Employees have varying degrees of motivation when it comes to work, but there is no quicker way to disengaging a large portion (if not all) of your team than not fostering a community of recognition. While being recognized may or may not be important to you personally, for your team members it's critically important.

Throughout my career, sure, I wanted to get a shout out when I completed a big project and winning money awards for great work were awesome, but recognition was never a driving factor for my own engagement at work. When I started to lead teams, it was something that I had to learn almost painfully, because it was not natural for me to pause for recognition as an activity. Part of that learning came through skip-level and one-on-one meetings and presented as not being sure if I was happy with their performance (because there wasn't a formal way to be recognized).

There wasn't a corporate program that we were allowed to use and I couldn't influence that, but I knew that I had to create something for my team. Even if it couldn't be about money, my team wanted to be recognized. I created a robust recognition system that, at its core, was focused on inter-team recognition across all levels through an online high-five. I then highlighted each submission during our all employee meetings. It was very popular and continues to this day, eight plus years later.

You'd think I learned my lesson from that experience, but I didn't. I didn't realize what my own language of recognition was until I was consulting with a company that had a very different standard of communication. Quickly I realized that my recognition button is to acknowledge my work with two words: *thank you.* Not a big announcement, it doesn't have to be public, and I don't even need to get credit. But I would like to know that you know that it was accomplished and that it's officially done.

This client doesn't have a thank-you culture. To me, it feels like it's common decency to say thank you when people deliver deep work and big projects, but at this company, they don't care to take the time.

I share these two stories with you—one from a leader perspective and one from an employee perspective—to remind you: don't make assumptions about recognition, and know that a takeaway may uncover new buttons. The best way to solve for this is to ask each employee how they like to be recognized (other than money). Keep a list right alongside their communication preferences and start recognizing them accordingly. Ask your team what's needed, what's missing, and what could be better. Then try a few things out and see if your team is feeling more connected with how their own performance is going—and with the team's success.

Setting Expectations

We've previously reviewed goal-setting and expectations, and how important they are to create the ideal employee experience. As a leader, this responsibility falls squarely on you, which can be a heavy burden. Regardless whether your company has a great or terrible goal-setting process, creating a team in which you're all tracking toward the same outcome and providing clear expectations is a practice that is well worth the effort.

Setting expectations is not just about goals, but also about the expected behaviors you want to foster within your team. For example, what is the expectation of response time when you receive an email? Are "thanks" and recognition required—and, if so, how and when? How is your vacation policy applied to the team? When should someone escalate an issue? What kind of language do you use as a team? And so on.

Yes, helping all of your team members clearly understand what is expected from them from a performance perspective is an important component of your team's overall experience and achievements, but it's also important to be clear about what kind of personal interactions and expectations, as team members, are acceptable. By setting these expectations and communicating them in an ongoing basis, you're able to provide consistency and safety for your team. If this happens, then that happens: an expected outcome. And it will support team members in knowing what is outside of bounds and know that it will be addressed—safety.

This is uncomfortable for many us, as in general we don't want to address negative things or question our own sense of expectations of what's right or just over the line. But not being clear around your expectations will create its own set of expectations.

In a previous role, my team collaborated with many different departments across the organization. As such, we got to know their own cultures pretty well. There were two teams that were always dreaded partners. As I paid attention to this, I started to interact with them more myself to dig a little deeper, and the team's disconnect was rooted in their stated and unstated expectations for their team.

One team in particular created what felt like an abusive environment for their team. The leader was beyond a micromanager. He was also condescending, chauvinistic, and a jerk. Through his own actions and what was acceptable for him, his team mirrored a lot of these characteristics when getting their work done. They had unrealistic expectations around everything: time line, responsibilities, outcomes, and so forth. And they were rude when they didn't get their way. They competed with each other, when there was nothing to compete about, and in general it was a toxic team. I really liked working with one leader on the team. He was kind, was helpful, and did great work. And then we had an in-person meeting with his boss in the room, and everything changed. He didn't speak up—because every time he tried answering a question, his boss shot him down or belittled him in front of everyone. You could visibly see him shrink into himself, and he stopped participating—as did his colleagues, because the expectation the leader set was that his voice was the only important one in the room.

This sounds like an extreme example, but think back to a team that you've been on or worked with that felt toxic or off. Maybe you walked away thinking, "How do they get away with that?" or "How do they still have a job (or keep getting promoted)?" (my often-thought question). The answer is that their behavior has been deemed okay and acceptable by their leader. And perhaps, their leader is the worst offender.

Setting expectations around goals and behaviors is critically important for creating an environment in which your employees can thrive. If this is broken or unclear, everything else breaks as negative moments will quickly outweigh the positive ones. This is also *why* so many people can't stand their boss (or say they leave "because of their boss"). It may not be about the person at all, but rather what they, as the leader, allow the environment to be.

Work Environment

Work environment can be defined through many lenses. We're focusing on the physical and the emotional environments, as they are the biggest influences in the employee experience. The physical environment means the actual workspace and location where your employees work. The emotional environment is a bit more subjective, but it's the overall well-being and mental state the environment fosters. Both of these are important, but in different ways.

Physical Environment

Our workspace is often the space we spend the most time in, in an ongoing basis. How it looks and feels is important, as we are in it a lot. You likely don't have a lot of influence around the office layout, colors, location, and so on. As long as you're supportive of your employees having comfortable and ergonomically correct furniture, and the like, you're doing what you can.

This is why supporting your team to make their space their own is the best thing you can do here. A new leader got his first office and was excited to decorate it to make it feel comfortable and a safe space for him. His previous job was at Disney—a lifelong dream of his—and he was a huge fan with lots of interesting Disney trinkets. He came in over the weekend to set up his new office; he filled with Disney trinkets, memories, and things that made him smile.

His boss was not amused. He started to comment on how cluttered it looked and how juvenile it was—and questioning if he made a mistake in promoting the new manager and if he was mature enough to lead a team. It was ongoing and relentless. The new manager felt like he had no other choice but to "redecorate" his office by removing all of the personalization. He was demoralized, and felt incompetent and undermined as a new leader. As a person, he felt disrespected, unsafe, and unaccepted. All because his boss wasn't into the same office décor that he was into.

People should be able to have personal touches around them. Of course, there are varying degrees of acceptability set by the company, but don't let your own biases get in the way of your team creating a workspace that brings them joy and positive experiences while at work.

This leads me to virtual roles. I am a huge proponent of letting your employees work virtually or remotely. There are very few office jobs that can't be done effectively from any location these days. Yes, working virtually is not for everyone—but neither is working in an office. From a physical environment perspective, being able to be 100% in control of your workspace can greatly impact productivity and safety—not to mention how much time can be saved in commuting! Consider virtual or telecommuting options as part of your work environment plan, especially if your team has to "hot desk" (find an open desk to work each day when they arrive) or aren't able to claim actual desks/cubicles/offices, as their own space.

Emotional Environment

In a nutshell, this is what will drive your employees to burnout quicker than anything else. The pressure, stress, and expectations around what needs to be done and when can be attributed to the emotional environment—along with feeling heard, seen, respected, supported, and safe.

So many things contribute to the emotional well-being of your team members, and you're not expected to be a mental health expert. But there are a few things that you can do to help support the emotional well-being of your team to drive experience and success.

Here are a few places to start:

- Respect their inboxes. Can you set a team expectation that you only email during office hours—or that, if emails come in after hours or on the weekend, they are not to be responded to until normal business hours?

- When they're off, they're off. Nothing gets my blood boiling faster than when vacation time is not respected. When your employee is using their vacation, sick, paid time off, and so forth, they need to be able to disconnect from their job. Let them—and create an environment in which emails aren't sent during time off, or, if that's too difficult to uphold, set the expectation that responding during time off is unacceptable.

- Trust your employees to do the work without having to monitor their time. Do your employees *need* to have their butts in seats and every minute accounted for, or can you relax a little and have them be reasonably available during set hours as long as their work is getting done? I'll admit this is one that took me a lot of time to get used to, but once I did, I noticed the morale of the team go up significantly. Some jobs just won't allow for this, but if you lead a team that does, can you be more flexible?

- Touch base. Do a pulse check, especially during really busy times of the year. See how your team members are doing, what they need help with, what feels like too much, what needs to be postponed, and so on. The trick here is to open the door to these questions, to help your employees feel supported if something does need to be readjusted. Most employees don't want to feel like they're, or be seen as, dropping the ball or not able to get something done, so if you're able to reinforce that it's a viable option, it will go a long way.

- Encourage breaks. People need time off and mental break, or even just a morning to sleep in or hang out with a friend or family member. Encourage your team to take time off to rest and recharge—and truly disconnect. It's not that hard to transition into this type of environment, but the positive impact will be long-lasting and well worth the effort.

As a leader, you have a significant influence on the employee experience. This is great thing, but it also means you have to be very intentional with how you set up your leadership standards. Your main role is to foster a successful environment while also not creating or reinforcing one that does harm. It's to remove barriers for your employees while encouraging them to feel safe to do their best work. This process takes practice, but as long as you're moving forward with your ideal employee experience in mind, you are on the fast-track to success—not to mention, being a great leader.

CONCLUSION

The employee experience is the single most important factor in creating healthy, profitable, and effective work environments and engaged employees. While it is a different approach than most of us have been using—so it will take a little bit of time and practice for it to become second nature—the results will be worth it.

Using the framework shared in this book—considering the four components of each action *before* you act or reviewing it to adjust in-flight—will have an immediate positive impact on your company's culture, not to mention your own career satisfaction and success.

While I began my quest in evaluating the employee experience based on my failed employee engagement activities, the results I have been able to witness, as an HR practitioner and with clients, have reinforced that not only is this the right focus, but it's also the easiest path to implement. Overall employee morale and increased engagement have been consistent outcomes by using this framework, in addition to providing leaders with more boundaries and less time wasted on work that wasn't adding any value.

In the beginning, you may feel overwhelmed by trying to implement all of the strategies and tactics at once. Instead, focus on one thing to get you started. The employee experience will greatly improve as you change one thing, and then as you move on to the next, your list of positive changes and experiences will continue to multiply.

Think of it in terms of saving for your retirement. When you add one dollar into your account a day, it seems like a small amount, but over a year, you have $365. Over five years you'll have $1,825. Over 20 years you'll have $7,300. The dollar value adds up over time, just like your experience improvements will.

And if the macro view isn't what drives you personally, consider how a simple focus or reframe on expectations or environment can dramatically change the safety an employee on your team feels—forever changing their life, career, and confidence.

Start small and practice taking the extra 10 to 15 seconds to consider the Employee Experience Framework elements before you move forward. Have you outlined your Know, Feel, Act, and Touch to determine success and set yourself up for success? These extra seconds can lead to multiple positive experiences in the experience bank—versus the unintentional negative experience that can occur without the forethought. That could mean losing a great employee, having a team member feel excluded, active disengagement, and more. It's worth the extra effort, especially as it will save you time.

Your ideal employee experience will be forever changing: as you update and improve things, as the work environment changes, and as employees become more aligned with the experience. That's the power of the Employee Experience Framework. The *what* or project doesn't matter as much as the components for your specific situation. It applies to everything you do, everything you communicate, and every leadership role.

If we don't change our focus from engagement activities to employee experiences, our workplaces will flounder. Employees will stop caring altogether and turnover rates will not be sustainable for productive (and profitable) businesses. Because of this and the stagnant engagement rates over the past 30 years, there is very little tolerance in the marketplace for Human Resources to continue along as it currently is: on the fast track to being superfluous and ineffective.

We still need employees as the backbone of our companies. Making things happen, getting work done, building customer relationships, and creating new products and ideas—even with more tactical work moving to AI delivery. By focusing on what we *can* influence, improve, enhance, and customize—the employee experience —we are able to build and strengthen the connection between each employee and our company: *true* engagement. Partnering with our employees to care about and buy-into our culture, our products, and our desired business outcomes.

Not to mention, as we are able to share measurable engagement results, each leader—in HR or not—showcases their strategic value and worth, while advancing people-focused leadership and solutions. Start small, practice the framework, watch the results through the eyes of your employees, and see the positive wake you're leaving behind.

The workforce as a whole, and each employee as an individual, cannot continue to thrive in a work environment that isn't able to fulfill their needs for the *next* 30 years.

END NOTES

Introduction

1. Lindsay Pollak. "What Are the Different Generations in the Workforce? Your Definitive Guide." Lindsay Pollak blog, May 16, 2017. https://www.lindseypollak.com/different-generations-workplace-definitive-guide/

2. Richard Fry. "Millennials Are the Largest Generation in the U.S. Labor Force." Pew Research Center website, April 11, 2018. https://www.pewresearch.org/fact-tank/2018/04/11/millennials-largest-generation-us-labor-force/

Part I

3. Jim Harter. "Employee Engagement on the Rise in the U.S." Gallup, August 26, 2018. https://news.gallup.com/poll/241649/employee-engagement-rise.aspx

4. "Facing Challenges Attracting Quality Candidates, Recruiters Are Embracing a Multi-Solution Approach to Sourcing." Monster, August,

2018. https://www.monster.com/about/a/Monster-2018-State-of-Recruiting-Survey

5. "2019 State of the Workplace: Exploring the Impact of the Skills Gap and Employment-Based Immigration." SHRM website, 2019. https://www.shrm.org/about-shrm/press-room/Documents/State%20of%20Workplace%20SHRM%20Skills%20Gap%20and%20Workplace%20Immigration%20Research%202019.pdf

6. "DNA of Engagement: How Organizations Create and Sustain Highly Engaged Teams (Executive Summary)." The Conference Board website, 2017. https://www.conference-board.org/dna-engagement2017/

7. Susan LaMotte. "Employee Engagement Depends on What Happens Outside of the Office." Harvard Business Review website, January 13, 2015. https://hbr.org/2015/01/employee-engagement-depends-on-what-happens-outside-of-the-office

Chapter 7
8. Ram Charan, Dominic Barton, and Dennis Carey. "People before Strategy: A New Role for the CHRO." *Harvard Business Review,* July–August 2015. https://hbr.org/2015/07/people-before-strategy-a-new-role-for-the-chro

Chapter 16
9. Tim Parker. "What Is a Good 401(k) Match"? Investopedia, November 10, 2019. https://www.investopedia.com/articles/personal-finance/120315/what-good-401k-match.asp

RESOURCES

The Employee Experience Solution Live Workshop
 If you want to learn the Employee Experience Framework and
implement it at your company while growing your peer-network, sign
up for our live workshop. Our facilitators will help you understand the
Framework and show you how to use it at your company, at the macro
and micro level, using examples and best practices. You'll receive one-
on-one coaching and support to ensure you're crafting the perfect
Framework for your company to get results. Register for a workshop
today at bettHR.com/workshop.

**Become Certified: Storytelling for HR and the Employee
Experience**
If you're interested in dramatically changing your leadership career
and trajectory by focusing on what works and executing the Employee
Experience Framework, apply to become certified in the Storytelling
for HR process. Those who are ready to shift their practices into the
future workplace, are welcome to apply. Corporations or HR
departments wanting to certify members of their team may also apply.
You can learn more at bettHR.com/certification.

Resources Mentioned in the Book

- HR Like a Marketer workbook: bettHR.com/hrlam
- HR Metrics: bettHR.com/hrm101
- Recruiting Brief template: bettHR.com/brief
- Repurpose content on a budget: bettHR.com/repurpose
- Selection Process template: bettHR.com/selection
- S/TAR template: bettHR.com/star
- Story Snippet template: bettHR.com/story
- Storytelling for HR: bettHR.com/storytelling
- Total rewards survey: bettHR.com/survey

SUGGESTED READING

Steve Pressfield. *Nobody Wants to Read Your Sh*t: And Other Tough-Love Truths to Make You a Better Writer* (Black irish Entertainment, LLC, 2016).

Donald Miller. *Building a Story Brand: Clarify Your Message So Customers Will Listen* (HarperCollins Leadership, 2017).

Greg McKeown. *Essentialism: The Disciplined Pursuit of Less* (Currency, 2014).

Simon Sinek. *Start with Why: How Great Leaders Inspire Everyone to Take Action* (Portfolio, 2009).

Michael Bungay Stanier. *The Coaching Habit*: Say Less, Ask More & Change the Way You Lead Forever (Page Two, 2016).

ACKNOWLEDGMENTS

First and foremost, thank you—the wonderful readers of this book. Without your support, this book never would have made it into the world. Knowing that there are people out there just like me, searching to create a better employee experience, even when it's hard to be the one "thinking too far outside of the box," keeps me motivated.

Thank you to my brother, Brad, who was cheering me on throughout the process and reminding me why this book was so important. You are always my biggest supporter and fan; I can't thank you enough.

Thank you to Kristin and Christie for helping me stay on track, clarify my ideas, and find more grace throughout the process.

Thank you to my family, for supporting me… even with you're not quite sure what I'm talking about.

To Jodi, for making this book better than it would have been without your editing expertise and guidance.

And finally, to all of my clients, thank you for the trust you put in me and my team. It's an honor to work side-by-side with you and see the Framework in action.

ABOUT THE AUTHOR

Melissa Anzman is the CEO and founder of bettHR, a leading HR consulting agency specializing in the employee experience. She is an HR practitioner with more than 15 years of experience delivering employee-focused solutions at several Fortune 500 companies across various industries including automotive, consumer goods, healthcare, financial services, and more. Melissa is a member of the Forbes HR Council and has two previously published books, *Stop Hating Your Job* and *How to Land a Job*. Melissa has earned more than 30 industry awards and her work has been featured in online publications such as the Amex Open Forum, Huffington Post, Forbes, and Business Insider. Melissa holds a bachelor's degree in Communications and a master's degree in business administration (MBA: HR Management) from the University of Wisconsin.

Get in Touch
bettHR.com
linkedin.com/melissaanzman
twitter.com/melissaanzman

www.ingramcontent.com/pod-product-compliance
Lightning Source LLC
Chambersburg PA
CBHW061206220326
41597CB00015BA/1537